Made in America

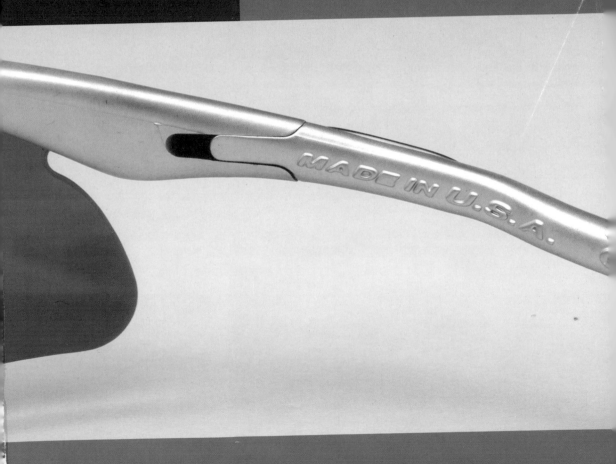

Made in America
From Levi's to Barbie to Google

Nick Freeth

MBI

This edition first published in 2005 by MBI Publishing Company, Galtier Plaza, Suite 200, 380 Jackson Street, St. Paul, MN 55101-3885 USA

© 2005 Colin Gower Enterprises

Colin Gower Enterprises Ltd., Cordwainers, Caring Lane, Leeds, Maidstone, Kent, U.K.

The information in this book is true and complete to the best of our knowledge. All recommendations are made without any guarantee on the part of the author or publisher, who also disclaim any liability incurred in connection with the use of this data or specific details.

MBI Publishing Company books are also available at discounts in bulk quantity for industrial or sales-promotional use. For details write to Special Sales Manager at Motorbooks International Wholesalers & Distributors, 729 Prospect Avenue, PO Box 1, Osceola, WI 54020-0001 U.S.A.

ISBN–13: 978 0 7603 2270 3

ISBN–10: 0 7603 2270 8

EDITOR: Candida Gower
DESIGNER: Phil Clucas MSIAD
PHOTOGRAPHY: Neil Sutherland
COLOR REPRODUCTION: The Berkeley Square Partnership
PRINTED AND BOUND: China

Introduction

The iconic products showcased in *Made In America* constitute an absolute smorgasbord of Yankee ingenuity. Taken together, these famous brands have forged a unique way of life for Americans of this generation, and continue to shape it. Their widespread diffusion across the world is also a significant indicator of America's cultural dominance. You only have to think of the Golden Arches striding across the planet to know the truth of that.

These products have not only sculpted our way of life, but have even left their mark on the American landscape itself. Glidden's barbed wire, enclosing and taming the great American West, and Otis's elevators, facilitating high-rise construction, have had a huge impact on the country we know today. Like stones thrown into ponds, the effects of many of the featured products ripple well beyond the wildest dreams of their creators. American colossi like Henry Ford, Thomas Edison, George Eastman, and Alexander Bell have fathered a world they would hardly recognize. Even some apparently humble products, such as the TV dinner and Tupperware have driven social change. Other familiar products, like the Stetson, have both a practical purpose and a deep subliminal message.

But perhaps the most wonderful thing about this cornucopia of Americana is its sheer eccentricity, with the juxtaposition of the sublime and the ridiculous. Wonderbra and

Wonderbread. Jello-O and Jockey Shorts. Groundbreaking products, such as nylon and Microsoft Windows, rub shoulders with the trivial and amusing: Silly Putty and the Pez candy dispenser. Each is treated with equal weight and regard. The book covers artifacts from every imaginable consumer category, as well as many great American teams and institutions. Iconic design, fashion, foodstuffs, leisure activities, automobiles, toys, games, tools, landmarks, musical instruments, home appliances, and weapons: they are all included.

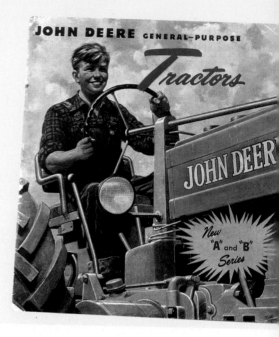

Behind each great product is an equally great story, and often a fascinating individual. The same virtues— toughness, creativity, and ingenuity— define many of the product originators. They often overcame failure, derision, and hardship to reach their goals. Colonel Sanders started his franchising empire at the ripe age of 65, funding the venture with his social security check. Poor Charles Goodyear was forced to sell the dinner service and feed his family from rubber plates. Monopoly had its roots in the misery of the Great Depression. While some were able to reap the rewards of their labors, others made cataclysmic errors of judgement that handed their success to others. The Hershey family ended up with their own town, while Ray Kroc reaped the success of the McDonald brothers' unique philosophy of customer service.

The single thing that all of these American icons have in common is success of one kind or another. In many cases, this continues to this day. And in some way or other, they have all helped to stoke the engine of the most powerful economy in the world. The sheer numbers involved are mind-boggling. Some of the featured brands belong to corporations whose revenues match or even surpass the gross national product of small nations. Just look at the figures for Coca-Cola and Starbucks. Their market penetration is also astounding. Mickey Mouse is reckoned to be the second most recognizable symbol of America, second only to the flag itself. But to us as individuals, perhaps the most absorbing aspect of the featured items is the impact they have had on our own lives. Certain products have the magical ability to transport us back to our childhood in the twinkling of an eye, while others are so intrinsic to our everyday existence that life without them is barely imaginable.

Although *Made In America* very interestingly points to a number of critical eras when many familiar brands and products were launched (the final quarter of the nineteenth century, the world wars, the period immediately following the Great Depression, and the mid-twentieth century), the book also demonstrates the ongoing nature of American innovation. The age of the genius entrepreneur continues, with the likes of Bill Gates and Jonathan Ive conceptualizing and developing products that we can barely dream of.

Our American panorama wouldn't be half so fascinating without the input of our consultants. Peter J. Frank of *Men's Journal* for honing the list of entries to reflect our design heritage. Joanne Hayes-Rines of *Inventor's Digest* for balancing *Made In America* to reflect our technological tradition, and James Flanigan of the *Los Angeles Times* for ensuring an East/West Coast balance to the book. We thank them all.

7 Up

Birthplace: St. Louis, MO
Originator: Charles Leiper Grigg
Hometown Now: Plano, TX
Date Introduced: 1929
Today's Price: $1.69 (33.8 fl oz)

Number of Products: Six 7 Up drinks
Brand Owner: Cadbury Schweppes
Brand Mascot: Fido Dido
Stock Exchange Symbol: CSG

Following his success with his "Howdy Orange" soft drink, Charles Leiper Grigg (1868-1940) introduced a new carbonated beverage in 1929. But calling it "Bib-Label Lithiated Lemon-Lime Soda" seemed most unlikely to foster brand recognition. Pricing it well above the competition (especially on the eve of the Wall Street Crash) also appeared unwise—as did Grigg's initial decision to sell it only in bottles, instead of making syrup available to soda fountains. Fortunately, Grigg decided to rename the beverage "7 Up" soon after its launch, and it became a massive, nationwide success. The "7" is believed to refer to its secret blend of seven natural flavors.

Did you know?

- The Webtender.com uses 7 Up in 247 cocktails, including "Axe Murder," "The Seven Veils," and "Whoop Juice."
- It originally contained the tranquilizer lithium, but this was removed in 1950.
- 7 Up's latest drink, 7 Up Plus, contains fruit juice, calcium, and vitamin C.

A1 Steak Sauce

Originator: Henderson William Brand	Carbs per Serving: 3g
Hometown Now: Northfield, IL	(Carb Well: 1g)
US Patent: 1895	Calories per Serving: 15
Today's Price: $3.59 for 5 fl oz	Number of Products: Six A.1. sauces
(Netgrocer.com)	Stock Exchange Symbol: KFT

King George IV's chef, Henderson William Brand, invented A.1. sauce sometime between 1831-34. Impressed by its tangy, spicy flavor, the epicurean monarch pronounced the condiment, "A1!" The sauce was introduced to America in 1895, when the trademark was registered. It soon became a true American staple, and is no longer part of the European food scene. A.1. experienced an upsurge in popularity in the '90s, when steaks and steak houses returned to fashion.

Six varieties of the sauce, including Roasted Garlic, Smoky Mesquite, and Carb Well, are now available. The sauce is now packed in plastic bottles, although the square glass packaging remains iconic. There are several recipes for mock A.1. on the web, but there is nothing quite like the real thing. As the manufacturer asserts, "Avoid grilling tragedies, keep A.1. on hand."

Did you know?

- As well as the range of sauces, there are now six A.1. marinades.
- Kraft's suggested wine partners for A.1. dishes are Zinfandel, Sauvignon Blanc, and Pinot Gris.

A-2 Flying Jacket

A

Birthplace: Hudson Valley, NY

Specification number: 94-3040

Date Introduced: September 1930

Number of Original Main Contractors: 14

Date Cancelled: 1942

Reissued: 1988

Spokesperson: Neil Cooper

Today's Price: $200–500

When the Army Air Corps officially adopted the A-2 on May 9, 1931, it was beginning an illustrious career that endures to this day. The jackets are still made to the original pattern by companies such as Cooper. The original specifications were for a "seal brown" leather jacket, in either horsehide or goatskin, with two patch pockets, epaulets, a shirt-style pointed collar, cotton lining, and knitted cuffs and waistband. Other details included the hidden snaps under the points of the collar, which were to prevent them flapping under the flyer's chin, and a nickel-plated steel zipper to keep out the draught– after all, this was still the era of open cockpit flying.

Did you know?

- Horsehide was chosen for the original spec because it was cheap and plentiful in the '20s and '30s when horse transport was being phased out.
- The A-2 jacket worn by Frank Sinatra in *Von Ryan's Express* was made in the studio's props department. It was handed on to Bob Crane who wore it in *Hogan's Heroes*.

Ace Comb

A

Birthplace: New York, NY	**Commentator:** Richard Marin,
Originator: Henry Goodman	Hollywood hairstylist
Hometown Now: Goody Headquarters	**Today's Price:** $2-50 -$2.99
Atlanta, GA	**Number of Products:** 11 combs
Date Introduced: Early 20th century	**Stock Exchange Symbol:** NWL

Henry Goodman immigrated to New York from Gritsev in the Ukraine. He and his son Abraham made a living by selling rhinestone-studded hair combs from a handcart, tramping the streets of the city. In fact, they were so successful that Abraham paid his way through college (New York University) by working on the handcart. The pair founded Goody in 1907, and, equipped with a degree in accountancy, Abraham served as the company president for fifty years. He finally died in 1981, and the company held a weeklong memorial celebration of his contribution to the business. As the business developed, Goody built up a greatly diverse product base. They are now the world's largest and most recognized manufacture of quality brushes, combs, and hair accessories. Goody is now a Newell Rubbermaid Company.

Did you know?

- James Dean used an Ace comb in *Rebel Without A Cause*—this resulted in a huge sales surge.
- Goody sponsors the National Spirit Group of cheerleaders.
- The "Goody Bag of Style" includes a 7-inch Ace comb.

A Airstream Trailers

Birthplace: Los Angeles, CA

Originator: Wallace Merle Byam

Hometown Now: Jackson Center, OH

Date Introduced: The "Clipper" launched January 17, 1936

Spokesperson: Dicky Riegel, President and CEO, Airstream Inc.

Original Price: $1,200

Today's Price: (Trailer) $29,894 to $86,653

Wallace Merle Byam was born to the travelling life. His grandfather led a mule train in Baker, Oregon, and he himself inhabited a two-wheeled donkey cart during a stint as a shepherd. He starting working on trailer designs in the backyard of his Los Angeles home whilst publishing a do-it-yourself magazine. He gradually perfected these, and launched the "Clipper" trailer in 1936. The Airstream legend was born.

The design ethos behind the Airstream is that it would be light enough, strong enough, and streamlined enough to tow behind an ordinary family car, on a "stream of air." This led to his use of the aircraft-inspired styling for his unique aluminum, monocoque shell. To this day, the panels are riveted together by hand. Once the blueprint was established, the trailers could be customized to offer five-star family accommodation, with the convenience and freedom of life on the open road.

> *"The country is experiencing a groundswell of interest in authentic American products ... and nothing embodies these qualities better than the shiny, silver Airstream trailer."*
> Dicky Riegel. President and CEO, Airstream Inc.

Since President and CEO Dicky Riegel took over the company in 2002, Airstream has enjoyed a complete Renaissance. Sales have doubled as adventure-seeking baby boomers go in search of the authentic American "road" experience. As Riesel says, Airstream is a "heritage brand" made "relevant to today's market." Airstream added the "Classic" motor home to their lineup in the '70s, and now offers fantastically luxurious recreational vehicles. The Airstream Skydeck, complete with a full-sized roof patio to entertain up to fifteen, can be fitted with all the comforts of home including a telephone, 20-inch stereo TV, DVD/VHS home theater system, and washer/dryer. A bargain at over $260,000!

Back to the great American outdoors. Making camp with an Airstream trailer.

Did you know?
- President John F. Kennedy used an Airstream trailer as a mobile Oval Office.
- Airstream trailers are on display in the Museum of Modern Art, San Francisco, The Smithsonian Institution, the lobby of MTV, and the Henry Ford Museum.

A Alka-Seltzer

Birthplace: Elkhart, IN

Originator: Maurice Treneer

Hometown Now: Bayer Corporate
Headquarters, Pittsburgh, PA

Date Introduced: 1931

Today's Price: $9.29 for 72 tablets
on Drugstore.com

Number of Products: Original plus
6 derivatives

Number Sold: 100 million plus

In 1928, there was a devastating flu epidemic in the United States that affected almost half the population. Hub Beardsley, the President of Miles Laboratories, discovered that some of the staff working for the local paper in Elkhart, Indiana, were taking a combination of acetylsalicylic acid and bicarbonate to relieve their symptoms and get them through the illness as painlessly as possible. Beardsley commissioned chemist Maurice Treneer to develop an effervescent tablet that combined these ingredients. The resulting concoction reduced the irritating effect of aspirin on the stomach ("Alka" refers to the reduction of the acid effect of the liquid) and made it possible for many more people to benefit from the medicine.

Did you know?
- Paul Margulies coined the famous slogan "Plop, Plop, Fizz, Fizz, Oh, What a Relief it is."
- Aspirin, one of the major components of Alka-Seltzer, was discovered in 1897 by Bayer chemist Felix Hoffmann.

American Express

Birthplace: New York, NY

Originators: William Fargo and
   Henry Wells

Hometown Now: New York, NY

Date Introduced: 1850

Income for Final Quarter 2004: $896
   million

Number of Products: Travelers' checks
   and credit facilities

Stock Exchange Symbol: AXP

The American Express Company was set up in New York on March 18, 1850, with the amalgamation of three express delivery firms, including Wells Fargo. Their early reputation was based on the speedy, secure transportation of letters and packages, especially high-value items sent between banks. Amex, as it came to be known, moved into financial services in 1882 by issuing its own money orders, and the first ever travelers' checks nine years later. The "Personal Card" came in 1958, and attracted over a million customers in its first five years. It was the start of a huge success story for the company, but its slowness in introducing a true "credit" (rather than a "charge" card) hurt the company's market share. Still, Amex remains one of the classiest cards.

Did you know?

- American Express headquarters was directly opposite Ground Zero. Eleven employees were killed in the 9/11 terrorist attack.
- "Don't leave home without it." Ubiquitous Amex pitchman Karl Madden spawned parodies on *The Tonight Show* with Johnny Carson.

A

AMF Bowling

Birthplace: Battery Park, NY

American Bowling Congress Founded:
   1895

AMF Enter Bowling: 1938

Hometown Now: Richmond, VA

First Automated Pinspotter: 1946

Originator: Fred Schmidt

AMF Employees: 16,000 worldwide

Owned by: Code, Hennessy and
   Simmons LLC

The American Machine and Foundry Company started out in New York in 1900, producing automated machinery for the tobacco industry. Like all healthy businesses, they diversified, and by the '30s, they were taking a great interest in the bowling industry with a view to mechanizing it. To reset the pins by hand took time and considerable effort by so-called "pin monkeys." AMF figured that if they could do away with this chore, it would revolutionize the popularity of the sport. The first public debut of the auto-pinspotter was at the 1946 ABC National Championship in Buffalo, New York. By 1952, the system was widely adopted. Coupled with NBC's coverage, this led to a boom in the popularity of bowling. AMF introduced the first automated scoring system in 1976 and the urethane bowling ball in 1981. This ball put incredible new power and performance in the bowler's hands. The company has sponsored the AMF Bowling World Cup for the past 40 years. Some 100 countries are expected to compete in the 2005 event, to be held in Ljubljana, Slovenia. The earliest reference to bowling in the United States is that of Washington Irving's character Rip Van Winkel, who awakens to the sound of "crashing ninepins." Irving may have done just this, as he was born near Wall Street, close to the first American bowling location in the Battery area. It is still known as the "Bowling Green."

Did you know?
- Bowling is the Number 1 participatory sport in America.
- AMF once owned Harley-Davidson.
- Bowling traces its ancestry to 3200 BC.
- 54 million Americans go bowling at least once a year.

*"Bowling is a lifelong activity.
Have fun and learn some things on the lanes."*
Bill Spigner, PBA Champion

- Many bowling lanes have now been upgraded from wood to synthetic playing surfaces.
- The number 1 bowling tip is to keep your arm swing loose.

A Apple iPod

Birthplace: Cupertino, CA

Originator: Apple designer, Jonathan Ive

Hometown Now: Cupertino, CA

Date Introduced: 2001

Spokesperson: Steve Jobs (see below)

Today's Price: $299 for 20GB iPod;
(iPod mini—$199; iPod photo—$349)

Number of products: 5

Number Sold: 3,000,000+

Stock Exchange Symbol: AAPL

In 1999, the first portable MP3 players—digital devices that store and reproduce compressed-format files containing CD tracks—appeared on the market. Most of these early units relied on memory chips, restricting their song-carrying capacity, while their appearance, though conveniently compact, was rarely very striking. The iPod, introduced by Apple two years later, represents a dramatic advance on such machines. Its computer-type hard disk greatly increases its memory; the first-ever iPod could carry up to 1,000 songs, and later models have enough space to hold entire record collections. Its elegant, lightweight design is the work of Englishman Jonathan Ive, who was also responsible for Apple's classic iMac computer. And the iPod's seamless interface with Macs and PCs, to which it links through its high-speed ports, makes loading it with MP3 or other audio files (either from CDs or Apple's online iTunes Music Store) swift and straightforward. In short, the iPod is a go-anywhere source of music that, in the few years since its launch, has become as famous and desirable for its unique styling as for its sound quality—and has amply justified Apple CEO Steve Jobs' bold 2001 prediction that "With iPod, listening to music will never be the same again."

Did you know?

- The iPod shuffle (the baby of the range) weighs just .78 ounces; a 20GB standard iPod tips the scales at 5.6 oz.
- In October 2004, Apple launched a special edition, custom-styled 20GB-capacity iPod named for the famous Irish rock band U2.
- The success of the iPod has spawned a growing range of accessories for the player—including protective "skins" and add-on loudspeaker units.

"*With iPod and iTunes, Apple has created a crossroads of art, commerce and technology which feels good for both musicians and fans.*"
Bono, U2, 2004

BAND-AID

B

Birthplace: New Brunswick, NJ	Original Price: $0.10 (16 strips)
Originator: Johnson & Johnson	Today's Price: $7.99 (box of 100
Hometown Now: New Brunswick, NJ	flexible fabric strips)
Date Introduced: 1921	Number Sold: 100 billion+
Band-Aid Trademark Registered: 1924	Stock Exchange Symbol: JNJ

Self-adhesive bandages were the idea of Earle Dickson (1892–1961), a cotton buyer for Johnson & Johnson. The company had pioneered the manufacture of sterile surgical dressings in the 1880s. At the age of 26, Dickson married, settling near the firm's headquarters in New Brunswick, New Jersey. His wife, Josephine, was a dedicated but somewhat clumsy homemaker, who had a tendency to cut and burn her fingers in the kitchen. The gauze with which Earle dressed her wounds rarely stayed in place for long—until he tried attaching it to pieces of fabric-backed surgical tape. The resultant dressing was sterile and stuck firm; it was also easy to apply, as Earle demonstrated to his bosses when he showed them a makeshift roll of his new bandage a few weeks later. They were sufficiently impressed to try marketing it, and the first BAND-AID bandages, produced in 18-inch long, 3-inch wide sections, appeared in 1921.

Initial sales were slow, and at one point, an executive at Johnson & Johnson's advertising agency, Young & Rubicam, commented dispiritedly that "not even a combination of sampling, advertising, and window display is sufficient to create a popular demand for BAND-AIDs." However, public interest gradually increased as different sizes of bandage were introduced, and the brand's profile received a welcome boost after BAND-AIDs were made available, without charge, to America's Boy Scout troops. Production rose further during World War II, while 1951 saw the appearance of *Doctor Dan The Bandage Man*, a book promoting first aid to preschoolers, every copy of which contained six BAND-AIDs. *Doctor Dan*, which was published by Simon & Schuster, written by Helen Gaspard, and illustrated by Corinne Malvern, was hugely successful, and BAND-AID's iconic status was assured.

Subsequent innovations have included decorated, all-vinyl, and antibiotic-coated BAND-AIDs, and in 2001, Johnson & Johnson announced that over one hundred billion of the bandages had been sold since the 1920s. Earle Dickson, their inventor, rose to become the company's vice-chairman. He retired in 1957 and died four years later.

"He picked the bandage out and held the two stiff pieces. And zip! that bandage was on the doll's head."

From *Doctor Dan The Bandage Man*
by Helen Gaspard (1951)

Did you know?

- Only $3,000-worth of BAND-AIDs were sold in the year following its launch.
- The first edition of *Doctor Dan The Bandage Man*, published by Simon & Schuster in 1951, ran to a record-breaking 1,600,000 copies.
- BAND-AID's annual worldwide sales are valued at about $30,000,000.

B Barbed Wire

Originator: Joseph Farwell Glidden

Birthplace: DeKalb, IL

Barbed Wire Patent Number: 157,124

Date Introduced: 1874

Barb Fence Company Founded: 1874

First Year Production: 10,000 lbs

1875 Production: 600,000 lbs

1877: Glidden Declared "Father of Barbed Wire"

Patented Barbed Wires: 530 plus

Joseph Glidden's barbed wire was the first product to make a truly cattle-proof barrier. It was this that ensured its success, and led to its dramatic effect on the American landscape and economy. Glidden's barbed wire was constructed from two zinc-coated steel stands twisted together with regularly spaced barbs along it. Glade patented his invention in 1874, then he and his partner Isaac Ellwood established the Barb Wire Company to manufacture their product. There were several challenges to the patent, but Glidden secured this in 1877. Enclosure with barbed wire had a particularly profound effect on the American West. Wood and stone were in very short supply on the plains, so enclosure with barbed wire was a practical alternative. But its effect was not entirely benign. On the positive side, barbed wire facilitated effective range management, farming, and settlement. Yet it also meant demise of the free-roaming cowboy and the open range itself. Practically, this meant that too many cattle were dependant on the dwindling stretches of public range, which became hopelessly overgrazed. In 1887, a combination of this problem and a terrible blizzard led to the loss of $20 million of cattle in Wyoming. Many Westerners hated and despised barbed wire, and it became known as "the Devil's rope." Nevertheless, Glidden's product remains the most familiar style of barbed wire in use today.

"A woman's dress should be like a barbed wire fence, serving its purpose without obstructing the view."

Sophia Loren 1979

Did you know?

- By the time of his death in 1906, Joseph Glidden was one of the richest men in America.
- Isaac Ellwood bought a 50% share in Glidden's business for $265.
- During the Spanish-American War, Teddy Roosevelt's Rough Riders used barbed wire to defend their camps.

B Barbie Doll

Birthplace: New York Toy Fair

Originator: Ruth Handler

Hometown Now: El Segundo, CA

Date Introduced: 1959

First met Ken: 1961

Original Price: $3 (now worth up to $9,000)

Today's Price: From $14.99

Number Sold: 1 billion plus

Ruth Handler, the cofounder of Mattel, took the inspiration for Barbie from her daughter, Barbara. The little girl made paper dolls and imagined them in the "grown-up" world. Ruth came up with a unique concept for a teenage fashion model doll, and she debuted in 1959. This first Barbie had a black-and-white striped swimsuit and her signature ponytail, and stood 11-inches tall. Initially, toy buyers found her unusually small and sophisticated. But soon a Barbie buzz grew, and she became the world's number one doll. Through the decades, Barbie has reflected a passionate interest in fashion, and her outfits have had wonderfully evocative names, such as Enchanted Evening, Portrait in Taffeta, and Silken Flame. The different Barbie models also have reflected sociological change and beauty trends. Tanned California girl, "Malibu Barbie," was launched in the early '70s. Black and Hispanic dolls appeared in 1980, and the "Movie Star Collection" at the beginning of this decade. She was joined by boyfriend Ken in 1961, and now has a whole network of friends and family members. From urban teen to fantasy queen, Barbie has been fulfilling the dreams of little girls and adults for nearly fifty years.

24

"My whole philosophy of Barbie was that through the doll, the little girl could be anything she wanted to be."
Ruth Handler

Did you know?

- Barbie was named for the inventor's daughter, Barbara. Ken was named after her son.
- Jackie Kennedy and Madonna have both influenced Barbie's clothes and hairstyle.
- Andy Warhol unveiled his portrait of Barbie in 1985.
- Barbie starred in her first feature film, *The Nutcracker,* in 2001.
- Many fashion designers have conceived outfits for Barbie, including Yves St. Laurent, Christian Dior, Versace, and Jean-Paul Gaultier.
- After 43 years as one of the world's best-known celebrity couples, Ken and Barbie finally split just before Valentine's Day 2004.

B Bass Weejun Penny Loafer

Birthplace: Wilton, MN

Originator: George Henry Bass

G. H. Bass & Co. Founded: 1876

Weejun Loafer Introduced: 1936

Bass Hometown Now: St. Louis, MO

Today's Price: $99.99

Number of Products: 16 Loafer styles

Stock Exchange Symbol: PVH

PVH CEO: Mark Weber

PVH Projected 5-Year Growth: 15%

Bass is the home of America's most enduring footwear standards, many of which it invented. Bass's most famous line, the Weejun Penny Loafer, was introduced in 1936. It is a low, leather, step-in shoe that looks a lot like a moccasin. "Weejun" supposedly refers to the Norwegian prototype for the shoe. Legend has it that the unique shape of the straps across the front of the shoe are modelled on the lips of Bass's wife, Alice, kissing each pair of shoes goodbye as they left the workshop. The Penny Loafer became a college student classic in the '60s (alongside white ankle socks) and sales of the Penny Loafer soared. Bass has used its heritage products, the Weejun Penny Loafer, together with its range of outdoor boots and shoes, to develop a flexible range of good-looking and comfortable footwear for men and women. Bass is now one of the premium brands owned by the Philips-Van Heusen Corporation.

Did you know?

- In the '50s and '60s, women often used to put a dime, rather than a penny in their loafers—the price of a payphone call.
- Charles Lindbergh was wearing Bass Aviator Boots when he completed the first trans-Atlantic flight in 1927.

Bazooka Joe

Birthplace: Brooklyn, NY

Originator: The Shorin Brothers

Home Now: The Topps Building, NY

Topps Chewing Gum Founded: 1938

Original Price: $0.01 per piece

Original Brand Name: Topps Gum

Original Logo: Atom Bubble Boy

Original Flavors: Grape and strawberry

2003 Company Revenue: $290 billion

Stock Exchange Symbol: TOPP (NASDAQ)

From its humble beginnings as a "change maker" (customers were encouraged to take gum instead of penny change), Topps has evolved a whole new segment of Americana. Topps Gum was re-branded as Bazooka Bubble Gum, named for Bob Burns's humorous musical instrument (the famous armament took its name from the same source). To promote Bazooka to children, the gum was wrapped in tiny comic strips, and trading cards were added from 1950. Ultimately, the popularity of the cards eclipsed that of the gum, and there is now a huge collectors' market dedicated to them. Even so, Bazooka remains an extremely high-profile gum brand. Modern cards have featured Elvis, the Kennedys, Michael Jackson, and *Star Wars*.

Did you know?

- The first Topps trading card characters were Hopalong Cassidy, African big game, Frank Buck, and All-American football.
- Sy Berger introduced Topps baseball cards in 1952.
- Sports card collecting may be the most popular American hobby ever.

B Beanie Babies

Birthplace: Chicago, IL

Originator: H. Ty Warner

Hometowns Now: Oakbrook and
Westmont, IL

Date Introduced: 1994

Number of Products: Around 22 new
Babies each month

Value of Sales: 4.5 billion

Brand Owner: Ty Inc. is privately owned
by Ty Warner

Ty Warner launched the first "Original 9" Beanie Babies in 1994. The line-up included Chocolate the Moose, Pinchers the Lobster, Spot the Dog, and Squealer the Pig. Warner had conceived the idea of an inexpensive toy aimed directly at children's pocket money. But the real appeal was the fact that each toy had its own name and birth date, making them instantly personal. Ty also sustained interest by constantly retiring Beanies from production and introducing new ones.

There are now over 250 Babies to collect. The slightly larger Beanie Buddies (Babies are usually between 8 and 10 inches long) were introduced in 1998, followed by Beanie Kids. The large number of retired toys means that there is a very active collectors' and trading market, and many Babies change hands on eBay. Country-specific Babies like Britannia, Libearty, Germania, and Maple are particularly desirable. McDonald's has offered Teanie

Did you know?

- Jingle Beanies were launched for Christmas 2001. They can be used as festive ornaments.
- Basket Babies, which had an Easter theme, were introduced in 2002.
- The tie-dyed Peace Bears were introduced in 1997. The nature of the fabric means that each bear is unique, and highly collectible.

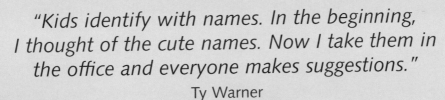

"Kids identify with names. In the beginning, I thought of the cute names. Now I take them in the office and everyone makes suggestions."
Ty Warner

Beanie Babies as premium gifts five times since 1997. 'Teanies' were a major part of the July 2004 25th anniversary celebrations for the Happy Meal. Beanie Babies have been so successful that they have also spawned a counterfeit industry, and several prosecutions have been mounted.

A pristine ear tag can double the value of a Beanie Baby.

B Bell Telephone

Birthplace: Boston, MA

Originator: Alexander Graham Bell

Date Introduced: 1876

Patent: #174,465, February 14, 1876

Bell Telephone Founded: 1877

First Exchange, Hartford, CT (1877)

First Long Distance Call: August 10, 1876

Company Now: AT&T

2004 Revenue: $30.537 billion

Alexander Graham Bell immigrated to the USA in 1871. He came from a Scottish family that were passionate about speech and language, and soon began to teach deaf-mutes. Bell's fascination with language led him an interest in the concept of transmitting speech, from which developed the basic concept for the telephone. He and his assistant, Thomas Watson, then spent several years refining the practicalities of converting ordinary speech into electrical impulses – to "talk with electricity" as Bell put it. They succeeded finally in transmitting the first sentence in 1876, with bell saying: "Watson, come here; I want you."

Did you know?
- Featured telephone is a 300, designed by Henry Dreyfuss. It was nicknamed the "cheese dish."
- AT&T, "Ma Bell's" direct descendant, invented the cell phone in 1978.
- Bell also invented the metal detector in 1881.

Bendix Washing Machine

B

Originator: Bendix Aviation Corporation

Headquarters: South Bend, IN

Founder: Vincent Bendix

Inventor: John W. Chamberlain

Sponsored Bendix Trophy Race: 1931-62

Bendix Washing Machine Introduced:
1937

Bendix Bought By Allied: 1981

Allied Bought By Honeywell: 1999

Stock Exchange Symbol: HON

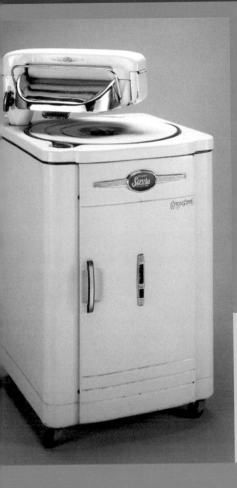

History is littered with inventions attempting to lighten the washday load. The first electric-powered machine was the "Thor" of 1908, invented by Alva J. Fisher of the Hurley Machine Company of Chicago, Illinois. But John W. Chamberlain of the Bendix Aviation Corporation took washing technology many leaps further in 1937. He constructed a washing machine that could wash, rinse, and extract the water from clothes in a single operation. This first Bendix was a front-loading machine. Swedish-American Vincent Bendix founded the company in 1929, and despite great business success, he was forced to declare personal bankruptcy. Bendix washing machines are no longer available in U.S.A, but the brand persists in Europe.

Did you know?

- 83 million machines are in service in the U.S.
- A gold prospector opened the first "Laundromat" in California in 1851. The 12-shirt machine was powered by 10 donkeys.

B Ben & Jerry's Ice Cream

Birthplace: Burlington, VT	Starting Capital: $12,000
Originators: Bennett Cohen and Jerry Greenfield	Number of Products: 50+
	Price per Pint: from $3.00
Hometown Now: Waterbury, VT	Parent Company: Unilever
Date Introduced: 1978	Stock Exchange Symbol: UN

Bennett Cohen and Jerry Greenfield both hail from Brooklyn, New York. They were born within four days of one another in 1951, and attended high school together in Long Island. Initially, they pursued different careers: Ben dropped out of college and later spent three years as a craft teacher, while Jerry worked as a lab technician after failing to get into medical school. By 1976, however, the two friends were sharing an apartment, and planning a move into the food industry. Deciding to become ice cream makers (they briefly concidered bagel production, but ruled it out because of the high start-up costs), and having taken a correspondence course in their chosen specialty, they launched Ben & Jerry's Ice Cream Parlor in Burlington, Vermont, in May 1978.

As Ben & Jerry's began to expand their brand, with its often zanily named range of flavors, it grew familiar across America and Canada, and spread overseas. However, the firm retains its roots in Vermont and still uses dairy ingredients from the state in all its ice cream products. It is also strongly committed to safeguarding the environment (its initiatives in this area include the decision, in 2001, to use biodegradable materials for its pint containers), and has given generously to charitable projects through the Ben & Jerry's Foundation, set up in 1985. Although Ben & Jerry's became part of Unilever in 2000, both Cohen and Greenfield maintain links with the business they created.

Did you know?

- The Penn State ice cream-making correspondence course Ben & Jerry took prior to starting their company cost just $5.
- Ben & Jerry's have been holding annual "Free Cone Days" at their Scoop Shops since the firm's first anniversary in 1979.

"If either of us had started [the business] on our own, we would have failed—or not been as successful."
Jerry Greenfield, *Entrepreneur* magazine, January 2002

- Ben & Jerry's best-selling ice cream is Cherry Garcia, introduced in 1987 and named after Jerry Garcia, the late lead guitarist with the *Grateful Dead*.
- Ben & Jerry's donates a minimum of $1.1 million to charity every year.
- In August 2004, the company launched its Dessert Emporium in New York's Times Square; the menu there includes ice cream, frozen yogurt, coffee, and pastries.

B Birdwell Beach Britches

Birthplace: Santa Ana, CA

Originator: Carrie "Surfin' Granny"
Birdwell Mann

Passed away: 2000 at the age of 99

Hometown Now: Santa Ana, CA

Date Introduced: 1961

Today's Price: From $38.50 (for a pair of Mid Thigh Basic Britches)

Company Motto: "Quality is our Gimmick"

Back in the '50s, there were no commercial surf shorts, and mothers sewed custom apparel for their surfing sons. Plaudette Reed, the wife of the City of Newport Beach Lifeguard Chief, was the first commercial surf seamstress making shorts from sturdy canvas. Nancy Katin was probably the most famous "beach mom" of the period, and "Kanvas by Katin" became legendary. Birdwell Beach Britches were the next company to come into the market, and are now the oldest surf wear company under continuous original ownership. The surfing side of the business began when Carrie Birdwell Mann joined her husband and son in their clothing enterprise, and began to make lifeguard trunks out of 10.10-ounce army duct canvas. The company has used Surfnyl fabric since 1970, which reputedly lasts an ordinary surfer for 10 years, and 2–5 for a lifeguard. Britches are now available in 40-plus colors, and various styles that reflect modern trends. Bigger and smaller pants have been introduced over the years to accommodate the changing shape of Birdwell customers; Vivian relates that the largest pattern they use is now 66 inches. The company has built up its business in a wonderfully personal and quirky style. Their catalog gently admonishes the customers to measure themselves properly and treat the products with care. Birdwell assures us that they can tell if their shorts have been worn for just 15 minutes. Reliability and style are the hallmarks of the brand, they "are comfortable and durable – and you don't have to worry that your pants might rip off – at a critical moment."

> *"We brag about our work, but we believe God has given us this business, which we never dreamed of having and we are humble."*
>
> Vivian, Carrie's daughter

Did you know?

- The little man on the Birdwell logo is called "Surfin' Birdie," named by Carrie Birdwell Mann.
- "Britches" was Grandpa Mann's childhood nickname, as in "too big for one's britches."
- Style 301 remains the most popular Birdwell garment.
- The company grew with "hard work, integrity, beautiful BRITCHES, and Faith."
- All Birdwell's products are still made in California.

B Black & Decker Drill

Birthplace: Baltimore, MD

Originators: Alonzo Decker
and S. Duncan Black

Hometown Now: Towson, MD

Date Introduced: 1920

Commentator: Ted Husting,
Sports Writer

Today's Price: $50

Value of Business: $6 billion

Stock Exchange Symbol: BDK

Above: The first model Black & Decker drill of 1920.

When Alonzo Decker and S. Duncan Black set up their engineering shop on Calvert Street, Baltimore, in 1910, it was an age of promise. The Blacks were responsible for sales and marketing and the Deckers for engineering and innovation. This turned out to be a good split. Among the products they manufactured at that time were a milk bottlecapping machine, a vest-pocket adding machine, and a candy-dipping machine. It was when they were asked to do some design work for Colt on their .45 automatic handgun that they were struck with the idea of designing a hand-held drill with a pistol grip and trigger control. Al Decker, Jr. began working at his father's business while attending high school, ending up at Cornell University's engineering school. On leaving college he went straight into the business, and his college studies gave him the knowledge to advance the company technologically. They developed the first cordless drill in 1961, and went on to produce a cordless rotary hammer drill for the Apollo moon program. Black & Decker celebrated their 85th Anniversary of power tool innovation in 2005 with a special edition cordless drill.

Right: The distinctive Black & Decker logo.

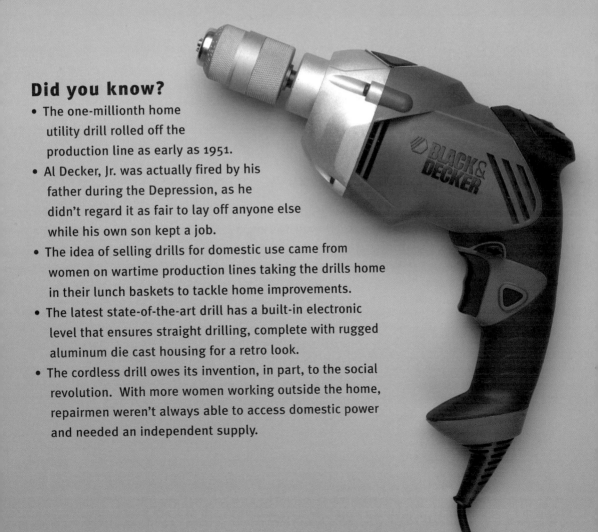

> *"The Army-Navy 'E' Award stands for exceptional performance on the production front of the determined, persevering, unbeatable American spirit."*
>
> Ted Husting, on presenting the award to Al Decker

Did you know?

- The one-millionth home utility drill rolled off the production line as early as 1951.
- Al Decker, Jr. was actually fired by his father during the Depression, as he didn't regard it as fair to lay off anyone else while his own son kept a job.
- The idea of selling drills for domestic use came from women on wartime production lines taking the drills home in their lunch baskets to tackle home improvements.
- The latest state-of-the-art drill has a built-in electronic level that ensures straight drilling, complete with rugged aluminum die cast housing for a retro look.
- The cordless drill owes its invention, in part, to the social revolution. With more women working outside the home, repairmen weren't always able to access domestic power and needed an independent supply.

B

Blue Note Records

Birthplace: Hackensack, NJ

Originator: Alfred Lion and
   Francis Wolff

Hometown Now: New York, NY

Date Introduced: 1939

First Hit: "Summertime" by
   Sidney Bechet

First vinyl 10": 1951

First vinyl 12": 1956

Stock Exchange Symbol: EMI PLC

Jazz record label Blue Note is now a division of the EMI Group's Capitol Records, but somehow retains its original flair and independence. It is home to a whole roster of classic and contemporary artists, including Count Basie, Norah Jones, the Reverend Al Green, Hank Mobley, Herbie Hancock, Tina Brooks, and John Coltrane.

Alfred Lion and Francis Wolf, German immigrants and jazz lovers, founded the label. They gradually built up the reputation of the label, always employing the "best players" to achieve a first-rate sound quality, blended into a unique timbre by their famous engineer Rudy Van Gelder (who continues to work for the company). Blue Note was also famous for making recording sessions enjoyable for the artists, and creating a warm and friendly studio atmosphere. Alfred Lion often picked up the players in Harlem, and drove them out to the recording studio in New Jersey, stopping to stock up on food and liquor. Early Blue Note fan Bruce Lundall is now president of the company, having first (unsuccessfully) asked Lion for a job back in 1957. The company fell into decline during the '70s, and lay dormant until the mid '80s when a resurgence of interest in jazz initiated a renaissance in the company's fortunes. They are now owned by EMI.

Did you know?

- Blue Note has been described as the "Heart of Jazz."
- The company began by publishing boogie-woogie piano discs.
- Reid Miles developed the highly recognizable graphic cover designs from 1956 onward.

"*There's something about Blue Note's mixes.
For their time, they are remarkable sonic documents.*"
Richard Cook, author of *Blue Note Records*

B   Boeing 747

Birthplace: Everett, WA

Originator: Joe Sutter

Hometown Now: Everett, WA

Date Introduced: February 9th 1969

Number of Variants: 9

Maximum Number of Passengers: 568 (400 Series)

Freighter Version Payload: 285,000 lbs

Today's Price: $176,500,000

Number Made: 1,381

In one of aviation history's flukes, the most iconic airliner of all time nearly didn't happen. Originally intended as a military transport airplane, the 747 didn't win the contract, coming second to the Lockheed C-5 Galaxy. However, Boeing was not despondent and developed the plane as a passenger jet instead. What became the "Jumbo Jet" was then the largest and heaviest passenger aircraft ever built. The distinctive hump on its upper deck made it stand out from the crowd. The aircraft's wide, capacious body made it relatively economic to operate in terms of its high passenger-to-fuel ratio. It could carry up to 600 economy passengers. This mass transport capacity opened up the skies to millions more people. By 2005, the plane had been in service with world airlines for 35 years and was still in production. The SP (Special Performance) variant of the 747-100 (pictured) was shorter by 47 feet. In March 1976, an aircraft of this type set the world non-stop flying distance record of 8,940 nautical miles.

Specifications: Boeing 747-400

Engines: 4 x Pratt & Whitney, Rolls-
Royce, or General Electric turbofans

Top Speed: 583.5 mph

Height: 63 feet 7 inches

Length: 231 feet 10 inches

Wingspan: 211 feet

Maximum Takeoff Weight: 910,000
pounds

Did you know?

- A 747-400 has six million parts.
- When pressurized, a 747 fuselage holds over a ton of air.
- One 747-turbofan engine produces more thrust than all four engines on a Boeing 707.

B Brillo

Birthplace: New York City, NY

Originators: Brady, Ludwig, and Loeb

Hometown now: Princeton, NJ

Date Introduced: 1913

Original Price: $0.05 a box

Today's Price: $2.55 for 18 steel wool Brillo pads

Number of Products: 4 Brillo varieties

Annual value of CHD cleaning products: $100 million

Aluminum pots were replacing cast iron cookware in the early twentieth century, but being used on coal-fired ranges soon blackened this shiny material. A pan salesman called Brady and a jeweller named Ludwig developed the original concept for Brillo. Their business partner, New York City attorney Milton Loeb patented the soap pads in 1913. It was he who coined the name "Brillo," from the Latin word for "bright." The Brillo Manufacturing Company originally sold its products door-to-door with the new cookware. At this time, the pads were boxed with a separate bar of soap. But by the '30s, the modern, soap-impregnated product that we know today was introduced. Brillo became instantly recognizable, celebrated in pop art, song, music, and movies. The size and shape of the steel wool pads has hardly changed since their introduction, but they have become softer, the (pink) soap is more effective and lemon-scented, and they now contain a rust inhibitor.

Did you know?

- Andy Warhol made his famous Brillo Boxes sculpture in 1964. Made from 400 oversized, silk-screened wooden boxes, it was his celebration of the "greatness of the mundane."
- Frank Zappa celebrated the product in his 1973 single "Camarillo Brillo."
- Brillo is now available in "Junior" sized pads.

*"I had incredibly good luck using a Brillo pad.
Everything was gone ... soap scum, stains and more!"*
Susan Adkins, *Cheapskate Monthly*

The revolutionary "Gripper"
was introduced in 2002, a red
plastic device designed to hold the pad
securely, while saving the hands and fingernails.

The Brillo brand name is now owned by Church & Dwight, which also owns the major household-cleaning trademark Arm & Hammer. The company is the world's largest producer of sodium bicarbonate.

43

Brooks Brothers

B

Birthplace: New York, NY

Originator: Henry Sands Brooks

Hometown Now: New York, NY

Famous Customers: John F. Kennedy,
Bill Clinton, and Theodore Roosevelt

Date Introduced: 1818

Today's Price: $44.50 Golden Fleece
Performance Polo Shirt

Product Profile: Corporate and casual
wear for men and women; boys wear

Brooks Brothers is America's oldest clothing retailer, and describe themselves as an American icon. Henry Sands Brooks was at the forefront of many important developments in menswear including the first ready-to-wear suit in 1845 (many of which were sold to gold rush pioneers), the button-down collar in 1896, the diagonally striped rep tie in 1920, and seersucker clothes in 1930. The company was both a maker and merchant, and they made all of their products easily identifiable with the introduction of the Golden Fleece symbol in 1850. Historically, the British woolen

merchants had used this emblem. The company introduced women's wear in 1949, offering ladies their famous pink shirt. After a brief spell under the British ownership of Marks & Spencer, the company is now in something of renaissance, having been returned to American ownership in 2001.

"To make and deal only in merchandise of the finest quality, to sell it at a fair price, and to deal with people who seek and appreciate such merchandise."

Henry Sands Brooks

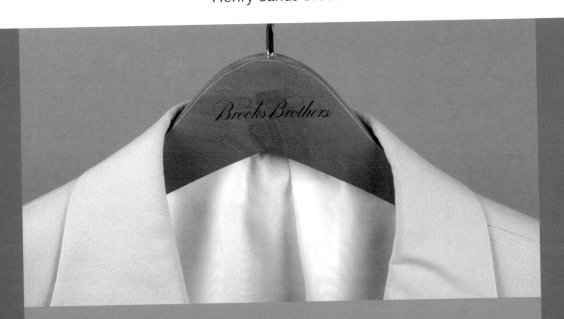

Did you know?

- In Greek mythology, Jason and the Argonauts were seeking the golden fleece, the Brooks Brothers trademark.
- Lincoln was wearing a Brooks Brothers coat when he was assassinated in 1865. The motto "One Country, One Destiny" was sewn into the lining.
- President Nixon preferred the "Brooksgate" range of clothing for the younger man. Truly!

B Budweiser

Birthplace: St. Louis, MO

Originators: Adolphus Busch and
   Eberhard Anheuser

Hometown Now: St. Louis, MO

Date Introduced: 1876

1901 Production: 1 million barrels

World Sales 2004: 116.8 million barrels

Barrels Produced: 1 billion by 1986

Share of U.S. Market: 44.5%

Stock Exchange Symbol: BUD

Eberhard Anheuser bought his first American brewery in St. Louis in 1860. **Adolphus Busch joined the company in 1864, and the company was soon renamed in his honor.** The company set out to create America's first truly national beer brand, which would transcend regional taste differences. Budweiser soon became popular, and was selling over a million barrels a year by 1901. Unlike many brewers, Anheuser-Busch managed to survive Prohibition (1920–33), and celebrated its end by purchasing a team of Clydesdale horses and a bright red brewery dray. The Clydesdales

have become an integral part of the company heritage and promote the brand across America. Budweiser now leads the premium beer category in the U.S.A., outselling all other domestic contenders. The company continues to use the original five ingredients of barley malt, rice, hops, yeast, and water—and is careful to retail its products while they are fresh. Every bottle produced in the company's twelve regional breweries is given a "born on" date, and an interval of no more than 110 days is recommended from brewery to glass. Budweiser has also done more than any other beer to change the profile of beer drinkers from blue-collar workers and college students to a diverse section of society, including women and professionals.

"The only major American brewery that's still American owned."

Anheuser-Busch TV commercial

Did you know?

- August Busch IV, the fifth generation of the family to manage the company, became President and CEO in 2002.
- The famous Eagle trademark was first used in 1872.
- The company's St. Louis brewery was declared a National Historic Landmark in 1964.

Bubble Wrap

B

Birthplace: Hawthorne, NJ

Originators: Al Fielding and
   Marc Chavannes

Hometown Now: Saddle Brook, NJ

Date Introduced: 1960

Today's Price: From $6.85

Annual Revenue: $3.5 billion plus

Stock Exchange Symbol: SEE (Sealed
   Air Corporation)

Al **Fielding and Marc Chavannes discovered Bubble Wrap by accident, when they were trying to** develop plastic-backed wallpaper. The pair founded Sealed Air and started selling the material in 1960. The material is composed of polyethylene encapsulating air. Bubble Wrap is now produced in several varieties, and with various "air cell" sizes between $\frac{1}{16}$ inch (micro) and $\frac{1}{2}$ inch. But apart from pink, anti-static Bubble Wrap, the material remains universally transparent.

Did you know?
- Bubble Wrap starred on the cover of *Playboy* in July 1997, wrapping Farah Fawcett's assets.
- The Museum of Modern Art, New York, featured Bubble Wrap in its "Humble Masterpieces" exhibition.

Burger King

Birthplace: Miami, FL

Originator: James McLamore
and David Egerton

Hometown Now: Miami, FL

Date Introduced: 1954 (Whopper 1957)

Original Price: $0.18
(Whopper $0.37)

Number of Products: 56 plus

Annual Revenue: $11 billionStock

Exchange Symbol: DEO

Burger King, home of the famous flame-grilled **Whopper since 1957,** is the second biggest hamburger chain in the world, with around 10,500 outlets and 360,000 plus employees. Since 1961, the business has been largely based on franchising, with over 80 percent of their restaurants owner-operated. Their famous slogan "Have it Your Way" is demonstrated by the fact that as of April 1, 1998, the sandwich may now be ordered in a left-handed version to better serve the 13 per cent of Americans that are left-handed. As Jim Watkins, Senior Vice President for Marketing says, "We have always been proud that we offered 1,024 ways to order our flagship Whopper sandwich. Now we are offering 1,025 ways." Of course, the menu is now far more diverse than when the chain began in 1954, with many salads, a breakfast menu, and kids meals.

Did you know?

- Burger King opened its 10,000th franchise in Sydney, Australia, in 1998.
- Burger King has outlets in all 50 states and in 61 different countries.
- The left-handed sandwich was an April Fool joke!

B Burma Shave Signs

Birthplace: Minneapolis, MN

Originator: Allan Odell

Date Introduced: 1925

Investment Capital: $200

Maximum Number of Signs: 7,000

Total Number of Burma Rhymes: 600

Sign Size: 36 inches long

Spokesperson: Senator Bob Dole

Original Price (Burma Shave): $0.35 for a big tube

Allan Odell conceived the Burma Shave signs to advertising the brushless shave cream made by the family business, the Burma Vita Corporation. Clinton Odell gave his sons Allan and Leonard $200 to purchase scrap lumber, and they began to position the signs along the highways. Originally, the signs were purely promotional, but they became more whimsical and humorous, imparting safety tips and homespun wisdom. Gradually, the signs came to rhyme, and became more uniform in style. Typically, they were painted red with white text, were grouped in fives or sixes, and were placed approximately a hundred feet apart. They became part of the American landscape and 7,000 were distributed coast-to-coast. But in the 1960s, big billboards superseded the Burma Shave signs, and it is said that the new generation of cars were moving too fast to read them. Ultimately, Philip Morris bought the company.

Did you know?

- The Burma signs advertising strategy was so successful that the brand peaked during the Great Depression, when it sold $3 million tubes of shave cream a year.
- Hunters used the signs for target practice in rural areas.

"*Growing up in the high plains of Kansas during the Dust Bowl years, I still remember the signs. They were as much a part of the scenery as the wheat fields and cattle.*"

Senator Bob Dole

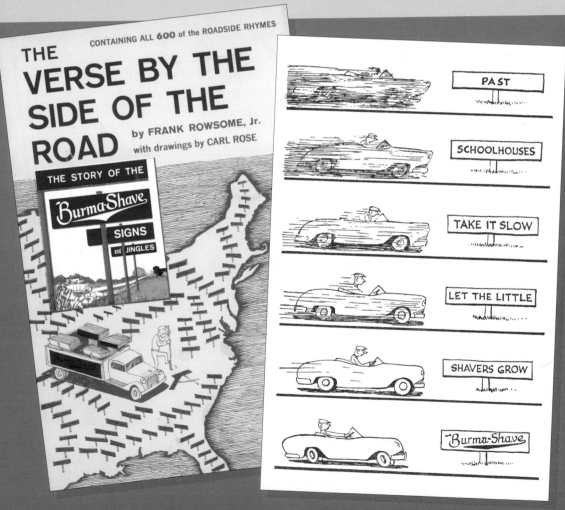

B Burton Snowboards

Birthplace: Londonderry, VT

Originator: Jake Burton, "not the patron saint of snowboarding"

Date Introduced: 1977

Hometown Now: Burlington, VT

Early Pioneer: Vern Wicklund

Date Wicklund Board Launched: 1939

Price Range: $49.99–$900

Motto: "Burton Snowboards is a rider driven company."

Jake Burton always wanted a surfboard for Christmas. Luckily, as it turned out, he never got his wish. Growing up in Cedarhurst, New York, he turned his thoughts away from nearby Atlantic Beach and headed for the Birch Hill ski area instead. His knowledge of skiing led him to experiment with the "snurfer," equipment for where surf meets snow. Both of these sports share challenges, which maintain a good deal of compatibility between them. Even then snowboards weren't new; examples are known to survive from the '20s and film footage survives from the '30s. But it is probably the development of the modern surf/

Did you know?
- Jake's trip to Europe resulted in steel edges and P-Tex bases for his boards.
- The company wasn't always successful and early trading losses topped $100,000.
- Burton created the "Chill" program in 1995 in order to help disadvantaged youth across America.

"If the board says Jake Burton carpenter on it, I jigsawed it."
Founder, Jake Burton, of his early boards

skateboard and advances in skiing technology that has made snowboards truly functional. Increased leisure time also means that more people have the opportunity and desire to participate in the sport. This has all added up to snowboarding coming of age as a real sport. Jake started up Burton in 1977 in Londonderry, Vermont, and got off to slightly shaky start. Lack of investment in those tough, first years meant that he had to turn his hand to anything—including roughing out, finishing, and painting the boards. These were mostly crafted out of wood. Burton also experimented with foam core and fiberglass wrapped boards. The company's mission statement reflects a tough approach to both of their main challenges: driving the business forward and participating in the sport itself. The "we wreck ourselves day in, day out" approach in trying to achieve a successful trick or the right line is inspirational indeed. The payoff for this commitment has resulted in a sport that was officially recognized at the 1998 Olympics. In 2002, three Burton pro-riders won medals at the Salt Lake City Winter Olympic Games. Burton itself has grown from a home-run company to a global brand.

Cadillac Eldorado

C

Birthplace: Detroit, MI

Originator: Harley Earl

Hometown Now: Detroit, MI

Date Introduced: 1953

Spokesperson: Bill Mitchell

Origional Price: $7,401

Today's Price: $68,000

Body Styles: Hardtop, Convertible

Number Sold in 1959: 2,295

Stock Exchange Symbol: XGM

The postwar years were good ones for Cadillac, and the company competed effectively with Packard for the luxury end of the American car market. By 1950, it was outselling all the other prestige marques.

The Eldorado was introduced in 1953, but like all Cadillacs, was re-designed and re-blended almost every year of its production. In 1959, the prevailing automotive styling was known as "Wurlitzer Jukebox"—and Cadillac was its supreme proponent. In a time of excess, the Eldorado still managed to out-glitz and out-chrome all its rivals. But at $7,400, it was highly expensive, and attracted only 2,295 well-heeled customers.

Designed by the outgoing Head of Styling at GM, Harley Earl, as his swan song before his departure later that year, the car was lower than its 1958 predecessor, but it was the body styling that really identified it. The towering tailfins were the largest ever to appear on a Cadillac, and together with the bullet taillights and other details, they clearly reflected the national fascination with the space race. Contemporaries thought that the car looked positively "Martian." Some people criticized the Eldos for poor handling. But at nearly nineteen feet in length, the "Batmobile" had been intended for good looks and luxurious cruising, rather than hard driving. Despite this, it could

achieve 0–60 mph in eleven seconds, and had a top speed of nearly 120 mph, courtesy of an enlarged V-8 engine.

Ironically, just as Cadillac's jukebox look reached its zenith in the '59 Eldos, the death of Buddy Holly, Ritchie Valens, and "The Big Bopper" in a single air crash signaled the end of the 1950s rock and roll era and of the flamboyance it had inspired. Nevertheless, Cadillac retained its position as the biggest manufacturer of luxury cars in the U.S.

"From a design standpoint, the fins gave definition … and established a long-standing Cadillac styling hallmark."

Bill Mitchell, Head of Styling at General Motors

Did You know?

- Cadillac was founded by Henry Leland in 1902, and was named for Le Sieur Antoine de la Mothe Cadillac, the French explorer who discovered Detroit.
- The company's trademark, aircraft-inspired tailfins, debuted in 1948.
- Though the car weighed some 5,060 lbs, it had a top speed of nearly 120 mph.

Campbell's Soup

Birthplace: Camden, NJ

Originator: Dr. John T. Dorrance

Date Introduced: 1897

Commentator: Lovemarks (website
dedicated to great brands)

Hometown now: Camden, NJ

Original Price: $0.10

Today's Price: $1.39 (Cream of Chicken

Number Sold: 2.5 billion bowls of the
3 most popular varieties annually

The Campbell Soup Company is now the world's largest maker and marketer of soup, and a leading producer of juice beverages, sauces, biscuits, and confectionery. But like so many great American institutions, the company had modest beginnings. Fruit merchant Joseph Campbell and icebox manufacturer Abraham Anderson founded the company in 1869. Originally, they canned tomatoes, vegetables, jellies, soups, condiments, and minced meat, but the business really took off with the invention of condensed soup in 1897. Company employee and chemist Dr. John T. Dorrance invented a method of eliminating the water content of soup, which enabled the company to retail Campbell's at less than a third the price of the competition.

Campbell himself sold the first cans of condensed soup from a horse-drawn wagon, but the company soon became aware of the potential of advertising. Its first ads appeared on New York City streetcars in 1899. Slogans like "M'm!

> *"My ultimate comfort food is Campbell's soup...
> it was immortalized by Andy Warhol but that was simply
> a recognition of its permanent place as an icon."*
>
> Robyn Switzerland, Lovemarks website

M'm! Good!" and the Campbell's Kids (who turned 100 in 2004) have entered the collective consciousness.

The fact that condensed soup can also be used as a cooking ingredient has been a great part of the product's success. Over 440 million cans a year are used in home cookery. Campbell published *Helps for the Hostess* in 1918, and continues to offer a wide range of recipes to the hard-pressed homemaker.

Campbell's soup is now offered in several varieties, including "Chunky," "Home-Cookin'," and "Simply Home."

Did you know?

- Many celebrities have endorsed the brand, including Ronald Reagan, Johnny Carson, and Orson Welles.
- Campbell produces regional soup varieties, such as "Watercress and Duck-Gizzard" for China. Kosher Campbell's soup is also now available.
- Andy Warhol's paintings of Campbell's soup cans raised the product to iconic status.

Calvin Klein

C

Birthplace: New York, NY

Designer: Calvin Richard Klein

Hometown Now: New York, NY

Label Launched: 1968

Business Partner: Barry Schwartz

1998 Underwear Sales: 30 million pairs

Brand Owner: Phillips-Van Heusen Corporation

Stock Exchange Symbol: PVH

Calvin Klein's name is now a globally recognized brand, adorning everything from underwear to perfume and cosmetics. Yet, his beginnings in the fashion industry were modest. Five years after graduating from New York's Fashion Institute of Technology (at the young age of 20), Calvin began his own company making coats. Within just one year, he had had a *Vogue* cover and started to produce casual wear with a wholesome, all-American look. His was the first label to retail designer jeans at affordable prices. He launched his line of men's designer underwear in 1982, which is now the most popular in the world. Brooke Shields launched his women's underwear line in 1979, with her famous line, "nothing comes between me and my Calvins." Philips-Van Heusen acquired the company in 2002 and added Calvin Klein to their portfolio of luxury clothing brands

Did you know?

- *Time* magazine has listed Calvin Klein as one of America's 25 most influential people.
- He was the youngest designer ever to win the prestigious Coty Award.
- Calvin Klein has always used hot stars and models to promote his products, including Scarlett Johansson, Mark Wahlberg, and Moby.

Carhartt Jacket

Originator: Hamilton Carhartt

Born: 1855, Macedon Lock, NY

Died: 1937, aged 82

Clothing Launched: 1889

Carhartt Hometown Now: Dearborn, MI

Administrative Office: Irvine, KT

Employees: 2,500

Sponsors: NASCAR Crew #17

Company Motto: "From the mill to millions"

Hamilton Carhartt was a driven entrepreneur who even added an extra "t" to his name to ensure that he would stand out from the crowd. He began his eponymous clothing line in 1889, with specialist apparel for railway workers, as part of his mission to provide "original garments for the American worker." Most of Carhartt's no-nonsense work wear is constructed from the company's own invention, "Master Cloth." This is a tough and durable 100% cotton canvas, or "duck." The company also manufactures a range of denim clothing and jeans, also in the American tradition. They now offer an extensive range of jackets, overalls, vests, pants, footwear, and even children's clothes.

Did you know?

- Mike Delfino, the handsome plumber in *Desperate Housewives*, wore a selection of Carhartt apparel in the show.
- Since 2002, the Carhartt SWAT Trucks have been travelling the U.S. to promote the brand.

Case Pocket Knife

C

Birthplace: Little Valley, NY

Originator: J. R. Case

Hometown Now: Bradford, PA

Date Introduced: 1920

Spokesperson: Randy Travis

Original Price: $ 0.75

Today's Price: $49

Number of Products: 200 plus

Company Magazine: *Case Collector*

Owners: Private company

Some knife lovers will settle for nothing less than the chrome vanadium blades seen on the mini version of the famous Case Trapper. Made from a special formula of alloyed steel, this is the "original" Case steel. These blades are known for their edge-holding ability and easy resharpening. The downside is that it is less resistant to pitting, rusting, and discoloration than stainless steel.

W. R. Case & Sons Cutlery Co. started business in 1889, making it one of America's oldest established knife makers still in business. In that time the company has produced some of the most sought after and collected knives in the world. They are not only used as tools but are highly attractive to collectors looking to make sound investments.

Each knife of today's production carries the famous "XX" trademark as a symbol of the quality built into its production. This originated as a simple X mark, which was made on the pan holding the knives that had passed through the initial hardening furnace. When the pan was returned to the oven for tempering, a second X was added. Thus, "XX" meant that every blade had been treated properly and fully treated. The featured knife has the Yellow Synthetic grip, which is a popular choice for collectors.

Did you know?
- Dogs were encouraged at the knife factory and many workers had them at their feet while making blades. It was felt that they helped sustain a convivial work environment.

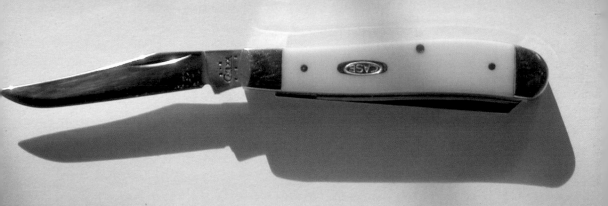

"*You're not just getting a knife, you're getting a handcrafted piece of history.*"
Randy Travis

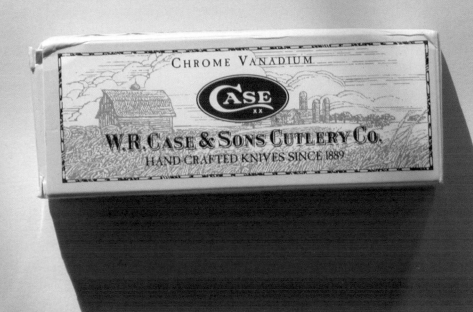

C Cellophane

Birthplace: Wilmington, DE

Originator: Jacques E. Brandenberger

Hometown Now: Wilmington, DE

Date Introduced: 1908

Original Price: Unknown

Today's Price: $1.29 for small plain roll

Colors: Candyland Crafts sells 8 colors

Dupont Revenue for 2004: $27.3 billion

Stock Exchange Symbol: DD

Cellophane was invented in 1908 by Swiss textile engineer Jacque E. Brandenberger, but the inspiration for it came from a different idea altogether. Brandenberger saw a waiter spill wine on a tablecloth and tried to make a waterproof textile by impregnating it with liquid rayon. This was much too stiff, but he noticed that a transparent film could be peeled away from the fabric backing. The patent for cellophane was acquired by DuPont in 1923, and they developed a moisture-proof version of the product. This elevated cellophane from a mere decorative wrap to an effective food packaging material.

Did you know?

- It took DuPont scientist William Hale Charch 2,000 attempts to make cellophane waterproof.
- The word "cellophane" comes from "cello" of cellulose, and "phane" of "diaphane," the French word for transparent.

Cheerios

C

Birthplace: Minneapolis, MN

Originator: General Mills

Hometown Now: Minneapolis, MN

Date Introduced: 1941

Number of Products: 9 varieties

Cheerios in 15 oz Box: 4,819

Number Sold: 1.8 million cases in introductory year

Market Share: 9 percent of all boxed cereal

General Mills, the largest flour miller in America, introduced "Cheerioats" in 1941. The cereal debuted as the first ready-to-eat oat cereal on the American market, and its first mascot, Cheeri O'Leary was introduced in 1942. General Mills abbreviated the product's name to "Cheerios" in 1945, and continued to vigorously market the brand, sponsoring TV's *Lone Ranger* program in 1949, and introducing the rather eccentric "Cheeriodle," a yodelling spokesperson, in 1977. Studies in 1989 and 1999 confirmed that oat bran could be used to control cholesterol, and that Cheerios are the only leading cold oat cereal to help lower cholesterol in a low fat diet. General Mills has continually added to the range of Cheerios on the market over its long history, adding Berry Burst Cheerios in 2003.

Did you know?

- Cheerios sponsorship supported America's transition from radio to TV.
- Children under five consume 23 percent of all Cheerios sold.
- *Scooby Doo, Star Wars*, and the NASCAR races have all promoted Cheerios.

Chevrolet Corvette

C

Birthplace: Detroit, MI

Originator: Harley Earl (stylist)
    and Ed Cole (engineer)

Hometown Now: Detroit, MI

Date Introduced: 1953

Origional Price: $5,675

Today's Price: $51,000

Number Sold: 20 in 1967 (L-88)

Parent company: General Motors

Stock Exchange Symbol: XGM

The Chevrolet Corvette was launched in 1953, and it was a huge departure from the norm for the American motor industry. It is said that GIs returning from WWII were the inspiration behind the car, as they looked for American models that reflected their enthusiasm for the British and Italian sports vehicles they revered—the Jaguars and Ferraris. Two men were the inspiration behind the car: GM Chief Stylist Harley Earl and Chief Engineer Ed Cole.

The ride to success was very bumpy for the Corvette, and it was nearly dropped by Chevrolet on several occasions. But by 1967, and after several styling changes, the car was an established part of the company's lineup. The funnel-shaped hood was introduced in 1966 and retained for 1967. The L-88 (pictured here), featuring a raft of specially designed performance-enhancing equipment, could develop 560 hp, and was primarily intended as a race-ready car for the track: anyone who tried to use it as a street car was destined for a shock. It was stripped of any of the normal refinements fitted to standard Corvettes, lacking radio, heater, automatic choke, under-hood cooling, and even reliable brakes; it also required special high-octane fuel to prevent engine damage. In fact, Chevrolet was quite coy about identifying the cars at all, in case the unsuspecting ordinary buyer might insist on purchasing one!

The capabilities of the car were demonstrated at the Le Mans 24 Hour race of June 1967, where an L-88 was clocked at 170 mph before a failed connecting rod forced it to leave the race. The Corvette L-88 was manufactured for a total of three years (1967–1969), and a total of 216 were produced. At least one of the L-88s was amongst a batch of complimentary Sting Rays presented to NASA astronauts.

"It takes high-speed travel over a variety of roads and through a combination of curve radii to appropriately reveal the car's inner beauty."
Car Life, August 1966

Did you know?
- Chevrolet described the Corvette as "America's one true sports car."
- Initial Corvette sales were so disappointing that the model was nearly dropped in 1955.
- The featured Corvette L-88 is owned by Bill Tower, a former GM engineer. He believes it was the first car in the series to be built.

Chevrolet Small-Block V-8

C

Birthplace: Warren, MI

Originator: Edward N. Cole

Date Introduced: 1955

Hometown Now: Flint, MI

Fitted to: Bel Air model range

Commentator: Brian Nicholls

Original Volume: 265 cubic inches

Maximum Volume: 400 cubic inches

Rating in Corvette ZR-1: 405 bh

Number produced: 90 million plus

By the early '50s, Chevrolet was stuck in a rut in the car market. Their cars were solid, dependable, but very, very boring. At a time when Ford and Chrysler were offering affordable V-8 motoring for the masses, Chevrolet was still plugging its venerable straight six. Even the sporty Corvette had to make do with this power source for its first couple of years. But Chief Engineer Ed Cole's mission was to provide the Chevrolet division with a groundbreaking new engine that would stand the test of time. His over-square engine combined a number of clever design innovations including thin-wall iron-block castings and stud-pivot rockers. The engine is still in production to this day.

Chevrolet's *red-hot* hill-flatteners!
162 H.P. V8 - 180 H.P. V8

Did you know?

- The small-block eight-cylinder engine, developed in just 15 weeks, was 40 lbs lighter than the old six-cylinder unit.
- The designers were so confident about the engine that they had ordered the plant and tools before it actually ran for the first time.

Made in America

"It looks good, sounds great and is easy to work on."
Brian Nicholls, Lotus engine tuner

Chia Pet

C

Birthplace: Bushville, IL

Originator: Walter Houston

Hometown Now: San Francisco, CA

Manufactured By: Joseph
   Enterprises, Inc.

Date Introduced: 1982

First Chia Pet: Ram

Number of Chia Pets: 10

Number of Chia Heads: 4

Famous Chias: 9

Walter Houston first created the Chia Pet back in 1975, when he used small pottery animals made by Mexican villagers to grow the first ever chia "fur." Still handmade, the Chia Pet is only offered for sale during the holiday season. Chia is the common name for *Salvia columbariae*, a variety of sage, which is almost unique in that the seeds become sticky when they are wet, which makes them adhere to the terracotta body of the Chia Pet. It is also fast growing—a Chia Pet can have a full head of hair (or fur) in two weeks. This speedy growth makes Chia Pets an ideal medium to teach children about germination. Chia itself has been an important foodstuff through the ages, and its very high protein content led the Native Americans to call it "running food." Today, chia is also used as a calorie displacer, which extends food without altering its original taste. A Chia Pet is included in the *New York Times* Time Capsule (housed in the American Museum of Natural History) alongside a copy of *Betty Crocker's Picture Cookbook*, a can of Spam, and a Purple Heart. The capsule is designated to be opened in the year 3000.

"Who needs a dog or cat when you can own a Chia Pet?"

Mary Bellis, inventors.about.com

THE SIMPSONS™

EASY TO DO...FUN TO GROW!

Contains:
- Handmade pottery planter
- Chia seed packet for 3 plantings
- Convenient plastic drip tray
- Planting and care instruction sheet

Chia·Homer
Handmade Decorative Planter

Did you know?

- The Cahuilla people of southern California grew chia as a food crop. Ground and soaked, the seeds were known as "pinole," and were a very satisfying food.
- In Mexico, "aqua fresca" is made by soaking a teaspoon of chia seeds and sugar in a glass of water.
- Xander gave Cordelia a Chia Pet to celebrate their anniversary in *Buffy The Vampire Slayer*.
- Aztecs used chia oil in body paints.
- Distance runners eat chia for energy.

C Chris-Craft Wooden Boats

Birthplace: Algona, MI

Originator: Christopher Columbus Smith

Hometown Now: Sarasota, FL

Chris-Craft Established: 1922

1934 Price: $495 for 15-foot utility

Today's Price: Up to $500,000

Number of Products: 9 models

Newest Model: Corsair 33 (introduced Summer 2005)

Number Sold: 100,000 (1922-72)

Chris-Craft was the first boating company to mass-produce mahogany runabouts and utilities. Indeed, it was their unique marketing and manufacturing strategy that enabled the company to become the

largest boat manufacturer in the world. Chris-Craft were deliberately aimed at America's burgeoning middle classes and their aspirations, and the boats were available on payment plans.

The company also realised that 90 percent of their buyers were not experienced boaters, but ordinary Americans looking for a fun and healthy leisure activity. So they emphasized how easy to handle the boats were. The company survived the Great Depression by lowering prices, and Chris-Craft is still in business as America's only premium boat brand. The hulls are now made from solid fiberglass, but retain their classic good looks. There is also a significant market for vintage Chris-Craft boats.

> *"The new Chris-Crafts are very high quality production boats, and their price tag reflects it."*
> Jim Shepherd

Did you know?

- Christopher Columbus Smith built his first rowboat in 1874, aged 13.
- The Dart was the first Chris-Craft racing yacht to gain acclaim.
- John F. Kennedy, Frank Sinatra, and Elvis Presley all owned Chris-Crafts.

C Chrysler Hemi Engine

Birthplace: Highland Park, MI

Originators: James C. Zeder and
   Tom Hoover

Date Introduced: 1951/1964

Fitted to: Imperial, New Yorker

Second Generation Fitted to: Charger,
   Cuda, Roadrunner and other models

Original Volume: 331 cubic inches

Maximum Volume: 426 cubic inches
   (second generation)

Chrysler has always had a reputation for powerful and innovative engines, and when the **Hemi made its appearance in 1951,** it was no exception to this rule. Innovative, because it was an overhead-valve V-8, powerful because of its advanced hemispherical combustion chambers, which inspired the "Hemi" name. The arguments over who actually invented the concept are legion (some claim that Zora Arkus-Duntov penned the design), but Chrysler was the first manufacturer with the foresight to mass produce the engine and use it in a range of their cars.

Other Chrysler divisions soon wanted their own Hemi variants. De Soto got the "Fire Dome" in 1952, followed by Dodge's "Red Ram" in 1953. In 1964, a second generation of the engine was introduced, a 426-ci unit. But this reengineered version retained many aspects of the original. This larger unit produced an impressive 400 brake horsepower, and found its way under the hood of some legendary names - Charger, Cuda, Challenger, Roadrunner, Super Bee, and Superbird.

Announcing the Hemi 426 Plymouth Belvedere

Now what this country needs
is a dragstrip with a couple of
good hairpin curves.

The Hemi-powered Plymouth Belvedere: a high-performance 426-cubic-inch hemispherical-head V-8. Dual four-barrel carbs. Dual-breaker distributor. High-lift, high-overlap cam. Special plugs, pistons and double valve springs. Low back pressure dual exhaust system. Blue Streak Special tires. Wide-rim wheels. Oversize front torsion bars. Sway bar. Added-leaf, high-rate rear springs. Firm-Ride shocks. And every Belvedere Satellite has: Front bucket seats. Center console with glove box. Deep-pile carpeting. Padded instrument panel. Safety-Rim wheels. 3-speed automatic or 4-on-the-floor stick, optional. Like an iron fist in a velvet glove, the Hemi 426 Plymouth Belvedere.

Plymouth ...a great car by Chrysler Corporation.

Did you know?

- The Chrysler C-300 of 1955, which sported the original Hemi, is considered the first Musclecar.
- Race versions of the engine dominated NASCAR speedways in the '60s.
- The Hemi was killed off by emission controls and high insurance costs in the early 1970s.

"*A competition engine capable of yanking Bob Fulton's steamboat over the George Washington Bridge.*"
Tom McCahill, *Mechanix Illustrated*

Coca-Cola

C

Birthplace: Atlanta, GA

Originator: John Stith Pemberton

Hometown Now: Atlanta, GA

Date Introduced: 1886

Spokesperson: The Coca-Cola Company

Original Price: $0.05 a glass

Today's Price: Variable

Number of Products: Over 400 brands

Number Sold: 1.3 billion servings daily

Stock Exchange Symbol: COKE

Coca-Cola is probably the world's best-known taste, and was the first truly global brand. Dr. John Stith Pemberton, a pharmacist from Atlanta, Georgia, invented the drink. He mixed the Coca-Cola syrup, which was combined with carbonated water to make a popular soda fountain drink, in the local Jacobs' Pharmacy.

The first customers, who paid a handsome 5 cents a glass, pronounced the drink to be "excellent," "delicious and refreshing." Dr. Pemberton's partner and bookkeeper, Frank M. Robinson, suggested the product's unusual name and wrote it down in his rather florid handwriting, feeling that the "two Cs would look well in advertising." The first ad for the drink appeared in the *Atlanta Journal*, and hand-painted oilcloth signs indicated which soda fountains offered the product. This was just the first step in a fantastic cooperation between the brand and advertising, which has made

Above: The famous logo is written in Frank M. Robinson's unique script.

the trademark universally recognized. A continuous stream of slogans have entered the collective consciousness, from "Drink Coca-Cola" in 1886, the iconic "I'd like to Teach the World to Sing" television advertisement of 1971, right up to the simple assertion "Real" of today's campaign.

From its original output of around nine drinks a day, Coca-Cola is now the world's most ubiquitous brand, serving over 1.3 billion drinks every day.

> *"The Coca-Cola Company exists to benefit and refresh everyone it touches."*
> Coca-Cola

Did you know?

- Coca-Cola advertising helped to create the modern image of Santa Claus.
- In 1985 Coca-Cola was the first soft drink consumed in space.
- Coca-Cola has originated a range of recipes based on the beverage, including French Onion Soup.
- Coca-Cola appears in countless films, including *It's a Wonderful Life*—there is a 1914 Coca-Cola soda fountain in Gower Drugs.

Converse All Star Sneakers

C

Birthplace: North Andover, MA

Originator: Marquis M. Converse

Hometown Now: North Andover, MA

Date Introduced: 1917

Chuck Taylor Joins Company: 1921

Commentator: Maryellen Gordon, *Glamour* Magazine

Sales Per Week: 30,000 pairs

Types of fabric: 11

Total sales: 580 million pairs plus

When Charles "Chuck" H. Taylor played basketball for the Akron Firestones, he appreciated the fit of a new pair of canvas shoes with high tops that he was given. In fact, he was so impressed that he toured the country promoting both basketball and the Converse range of shoes. The shoes were a product of the Converse Rubber Company, founded by Marquis M. Converse in 1908. Chuck used his basketball knowledge to help improve the All Star shoes, and added his signature to the ankle patch in 1923. Known as the "Ambassador of Basketball," Chuck's reputation was such that his endorsement of All Stars led virtually every player in the National Basketball League to wear the shoes. In World War II, Chuck became the fitness consultant to the U.S. Armed Forces, and the shoe became the official sports sneaker of the mobilized men. In 1962 a new low-cut version of the "Chuck," the "Oxford," was introduced. By 1966 this was available in seven cool colors. Sadly, Chuck died in 1969, when his beloved shoes were at the height of their popularity. The All Star is now available in an array of fabrics: canvas, hemp, flannel, leather, suede, nubuck, corduroy, denim, velvet, vinyl, and even gold lamé. The shoes are back in fashion right now, as part of the "post-pop-tart-punk" revival.

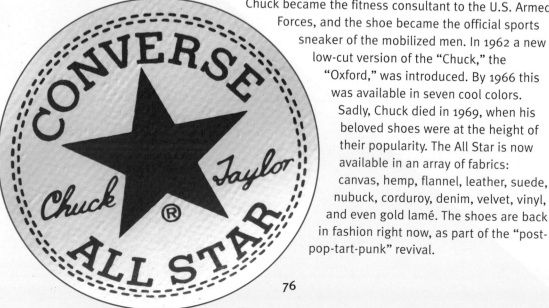

76

"They're a great way to mix high and low fashion."
Maryellen Gordon, *Glamour* magazine

Did you know?

- 60% of all Americans have owned at least one pair of Converses.
- Kurt Cobain was wearing a pair of "One Star" Converse Sneakers when he died.
- The shoe is 90 years old and still in fashion.

C

Coppertone

Birthplace: Miami Beach, FL

Originator: Benjamin Green

Hometown Now: Memphis, TN

Date Introduced: 1944

1945 Slogan: "Don't be a pale face"

1955 Slogan: "Tan Don't Burn"

Number of Sunscreen Products: 36

Brand Owner: Schering-Plough Healthcare

Stock Exchange Symbol: SGP

America's leading sun care brand dates from 1944. This is when pharmacist Benjamin Green invented in his Miami Beach kitchen the first sun-tanning cream, which he perfumed with jasmine. As "Coppertone," he launched a range of tanning products, together with a highly effective and enduring advertising campaign featuring the "Coppertone Girl." The company introduced their first sunless tanning lotion in 1960. As concern about the safety of sun bathing grew, the company responded to these fears by establishing the Coppertone Research Center in 1971. As a result, they introduced the 'SFP' categorization in 1972 and the first UVA/UVB lotion in 1980. Coppertone cofounded the Sun Safety Alliance and the Sun Safety Program.

Did you know?

- The three-year-old Jodie Foster advertised Coppertone in 1965.
- In its 2001 launch year, Coppertone Endless Summer became the best-selling sun care product in the United States.
- Coppertone introduced purple sun block in 1997.

Cracker Jack

C

Birthplace: Chicago World's Fair

Originators: Fred and Louis Rueckheim

Date Introduced: 1893

1912: Prize in every package

1918: Sailor Jack and Bingo introduced

1955: First TV advertising on CBS

Toys Given Away: 23 billion since 1912

Nutritional Information: 120 calories per 28 g

The Rueckheims' product was originally **called "Candied Popcorn and Peanuts,"** but when a salesman expostulated, "that's a crackerjack!" Fred immediately retorted, "So it is" and copyrighted the snappy name.

The delicious concoction of popcorn, peanuts, and molasses was immortalized in Jack Norworth's 1908 song "Take Me Out to the Ball Game," with the line "Buy me some peanuts and Cracker Jack." Sales of the brand were hugely boosted by the insertion of small toys in the original packages, which are still included to this day. Fat-free Cracker Jack was introduced in 1995, and popcorn-free Butter Toffee Peanuts were brought out in 2000. Frito-Lay, the convenience foods division of PepsiCo, bought the brand in 1997.

Did you know?

- Cracker Jack is the world's largest user of toys.
- A complete set of 1915 Cracker Jack baseball cards has been valued at $60,000.
- Sailor Jack was based on Fred Rueckheim's grandson, Robert, who tragically died from pneumonia, age 8.

C Craftsman Tools

Birthplace: Chicago, IL

Originator: Arthur Barrows

Company: Sears, Roebuck and Co.

Hometown Now: Hoffman Estates, IL

Range Introduced: 1927

Commentators: A.J. Foyt and Bob Vila

Sears Stores: 900

Sears Employees: 250,000

Length Of Warranty: Forever

The Craftsman brand came into existence when Arthur Barrow, Sears, Roebuck and Co's head of hardware bought the brand name from the Marion-Craftsman Tool Co. for $500. The tool market was changing fast in the '20s, moving away from the needs of farmers, who needed tough, basic implements, to those of a new mechanical elite, who demanded precision tools in which they took great pride. When Arthur was promoted, his replacement, Tom Dunlap, understood this transition and enhanced the design of the Craftsman range by introducing full-polish chrome plating. Sales shot up six-fold. Craftsman hand and power tools are now exclusive to Sears' 900 stores, and are ranked as the No. 1 brand for quality and value.

Did you know?

- Craftsman tools were used to build the St Louis Arch, the Statue of Liberty, and the Golden Gate Bridge.
- The machining tolerances of Craftsman ratchets have to be within four thousands of an inch before they can leave the assembly line.

Crayola

Birthplace: Peekskill, NY

Originators: Edwin Binney and
    C. Harold Smith

Hometown Now: Easton, PA

Date Introduced: 1903

Original Price: $0.05 (8 crayons)

Today's Price: from $1.49 (16 crayons)

Number of Products: 100 plus

Annual Production: 3 billion crayons

Number of Colors 2003: 120

Edwin Binney and C. Harold Smith had a background in color technology. Edwin's father had started the Peekskill Chemical Company and developed various paint and chemical products in the red-black color range. Edwin and Harold began their own partnership in 1885. They set out to formulate a range of crayons that would be specifically marketed to children—safe, non-toxic, and affordable—and introduced a box of eight "Crayolas" in 1903. Edwin's wife, Alice, had coined the word by combining "craie" (French for chalk) and "ola" (for oleaginous). Crayola now offers a huge range, including crayons that sparkle, glow in the dark, and smell like flowers. The company has been owned by Hallmark since 1984.

Did you know?

- Edwin Binney's father manufactured the famous red barn paint.
- Edwin Binney and C. Harold Smith were cousins.
- Crayola produced a series of Centennial Collector's Tins in 2003, filled with retired colors. Binney & Smith also owns Silly Putty.

C | Cream of Wheat Cereal

Birthplace: Grand Forks, ND

Originator: Thomas S. Amidon

Hometown Now: Northfield, IL

Date Introduced: 1893

Spokesperson: *Fortune* magazine

Original Price: Unknown

Today's Price: $4.99 (12oz box)

Number of Products: 11

Brand: Nabisco / Kraft

Stock Exchange Symbol: KFT

The head miller at the Diamond Mill of Grand Forks, North Dakota, invented Cream of Wheat when the business fell into difficulties. Thomas S. Amidon persuaded the owners that they should try to make some kind of porridge product using farina, the "purified middlings" of the mill. One of the partner's brothers, Fred Clifford Sr., came up with the name because the resulting product was so white. There were several hot "grainy" cereals on the market at the time (such as Mello-Wheat, Wheatena, and Post-O) but the pure whiteness of Cream of Wheat was very attractive at a time when this color symbolized wholesome, middle-class cleanliness. It soon became Diamond Mill's chief product, and is now produced by food giant Kraft.

Did you know?

- During the Great Depression, *Fortune* magazine called the cereal "A kind of Yankee fairy story."
- The company was one of the earliest exponents of heavy advertising for a low-margin, high-volume product.

Daisy Red Ryder BB Gun

D

Birthplace: Plymouth, MI

Originator: Clarence Hamilton

Hometown Now: Rogers, AR

Date Introduced: 1939

Commentator: Lewis Cass Hough

Original Price: Free premium item

Today's Price: $19.95

Number Sold: 9 million

Manufactured By: Daisy Manufacturing
   Company, Inc.

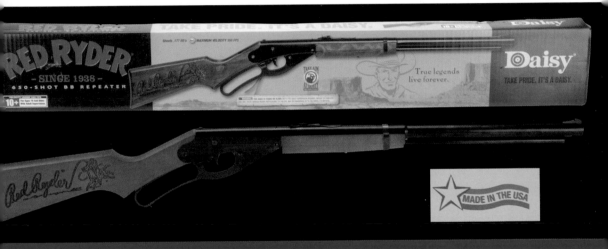

"**B**oy, that's a daisy!" was the reaction of the **General Manager of the Plymouth Iron Windmill** Company when he fired designer Clarence Hamilton's newly invented gun. This was 1886, and the company, which produced farm windmills, was looking to diversify its manufacturing base. The market for windmills was growing uncertain with the development of electric- and gas-driven machinery, and what started out as an incentive device (farmers were given a free air-gun with the purchase of every new windmill) ended up saving the company.

Did you know?

- Charles Bennett joined the company in 1891 as its first salesman, at a salary of $85 per month. His first trip to Chicago netted the company an order for 10,000 air-guns.
- The gun got its name from the General Manager Lewis C. Hough's outburst.

D | Disneyland

Birthplace: Burbank, CA

Originator: Walt E. Disney

Hometown Now: Anaheim, CA

Construction Begun: July 1954

Disneyland Opened: July 1955

First Day Entry: 28,154 guests

Original Cost: $17,000,000

Single Day Entry 2005: $53

100 Millionth Guest: 1971

Stock Exchange Symbol: DIS

Walt Disney originally conceived a small park for his studio workers and their families on an eight-acre lot adjacent to his Burbank, California, studios. But Walt and his brother Roy could see the great potential for the idea. Disney himself had been frustrated by the lack of facilities available where parents could have fun with their children. He believed that such a "theme park" could be a commercial success, and coined the name "Disneyland." Walt struck a TV deal with ABC to help fund and promote the park, which was to be themed around five concepts: Main Street, U.S.A., Adventureland, Frontierland, Fantasyland, and Tomorrowland. Disney relied on his studio staff to breathe life into the Magic Kingdom, and 160 acres of orange groves and walnut trees were gradually transformed into "The Happiest Place On Earth." The story of Disneyland is one of continual development and improvement, and the inclusion of modern Disney characters. The year 2005 marks the fiftieth anniversary of the park, and an eighteen-month long celebration, "The Happiest Homecoming On Earth" began on May 5. The newest Disneyland will be opened in Hong Kong towards the end of 2005, proving yet again how Disney's bold vision has stood the test of time.

Did you know?

- Walt and his wife Lillian celebrated their thirtieth anniversary at Disneyland in July 1955.
- Coca-Cola is one of only three original sponsors still at the park.
- The U.S. Postal Service launched a set of stamps, "The Art of Disney," to commemorate the park's fiftieth anniversary in 2005.

*"I could never convince the financiers that
Disneyland was feasible because dreams offer
too little collateral."*
Walt E. Disney

D   Dr. Pepper

Birthplace: Waco, TX

Originator: Charles Alderton and
Wade Morrison

Hometown Now: Plano, TX

Date Introduced: 1885

Today's Price: Case of 24, 12 oz cans,
around $10

Number of Products: 3 varieties

Market share: 16% of the soft
drinks market

Dr. Pepper is the oldest soft drink in America, and remains one of the world's favorite beverages to this day. Like Coca-Cola, the drink was originally sold in a local drug store. Legend has it that the drink was invented by pharmacist Charles Alderton, and named by drug store owner Wade Morrison in honor of his first employer, Dr. Charles Pepper of Virginia. But the drink really hit the big time when it was introduced to the 20 million visitors to the 1904 St. Louis World's Fair. The Fair also saw the launch of ice cream cones, hot dogs, and hamburger buns. Dr. Pepper was merged with 7Up in 1986, and the company was acquired by Cadbury Schweppes PLC in 1995. It is now the largest non-cola drinks enterprise in North America with about 16% of the market.

Did you know?

- Dublin, Texas, is officially known as "Dr. Pepper" for one week each June.
- "Old Doc," with monocle and top hat, was the trademark character in the '20s and '30s.

Duct Tape

D

Originator: Johnson & Johnson	Today's Price: Approximately $9.95 for
Hometown Now: Various	180 feet of heavy-duty tape
Date Introduced: 1942	Number of Products: Eight
Commentators: The Duct Tape	manufacturers making various
Guys/*The Red Green Show*	derivative products

What became known as duct tape was first conceived by the Johnson & Johnson Permacel Division in around 1942, and (as a green tape) was used during World War II to keep moisture out of ammunition boxes. Because it was waterproof, it became known as "Duck" tape. It became "Duct" tape, and silver, during the '50s, when the product was used to secure ductwork for forced air furnaces. But the true versatility of the tape means that it can be used for thousands of permanent and temporary repairs, as well as many other projects, creative and kitsch. In fact, a whole cult has grown up around the product, including such proponents as the Duct Tape Guys (authors of *Duct Tape is Not Enough*) and TV's *The Red Green Show,* which advocates the "Handyman's Secret Weapon," and "Spare the duct tape, spoil the job."

Did you know?
- A roll of duct tape is taken on every space shuttle mission.
- A Duct Tape Festival is held annually in Avon, Ohio.
- Apollo 13 astronauts made running repairs with duct tape.

Duncan Hines Cakes

D

Originator: Duncan Hines
Birthplace: Bowling Green, KY
Hometown Now: Cherry Hill, NJ
Guide Introduced: Christmas 1935
Hines-Park Food Inc. Founded: 1947

Purchased by Procter & Gamble: 1956
1985 Brand Value: $0.41 billion
Today's Price: Lemon Supreme $2.55
Number of Products: 22 cake mixes
Brand Owner: Aurora Foods

Duncan Hines worked as a travelling salesman for 33 years, which led him to eat in many different restaurants across the country. He soon became aware of the extremely variable quality of these roadside restaurants, and began to compile a list of his favorite "harbors of refreshment." He sent out a list of 167 preferred stopping places with his 1935 Christmas cards, and was amazed by the enthusiastic response it received. He extended the idea to a book, *Adventures in Good Eating* published in 1935, followed by *Adventures in Good Cookery* in 1939. He began to award "Recommended by Duncan Hines" signs, and became a highly regarded food critic. Businessman Roy Park approached him with the idea of endorsing good quality food products in 1947, the start of a famous American brand. Duncan Hines is now part of the Aurora Foods portfolio.

Did you know?

- Duncan Hines's first endorsed product, vanilla ice cream, was launched in 1950.
- Duncan Hines said that he had "run less risk driving my way across the country than eating my way across it."
- Florence Hines made notes about food quality, sanitation, service, and restaurant specials.

eBay

Birthplace: San Jose, CA

Originators: Pierre Omidyar and Jeff Skoll

Hometown Now: San Jose, CA

Date Introduced: 1995

Insertion Fee: $0.30–$3.30

Final Value (Fee): 1.25–5% of sales price

2004 Revenues: $3,271.3 million

2004 Assets: $2,911.1 million

Market Value 2005: $48.57 billion

eBay is a very unusual company, in that its "big idea" is to connect sellers to buyers, rather than selling anything themselves. Originating in Pierre Omidyar's San Jose sitting room, eBay was originally called "AuctionWeb." It is now rated as the fifth fastest growing company in the U.S.A. The concept of the web-based, person-to-person trading community is now so deeply entrenched that some people make a living from trading goods on eBay. The per-sale values of deals posted on

Did you know?

- eBay is *Fortune's* fifth fastest growing U.S. company.
- eBay describes itself as an on-line version of a garage sale, collectibles show, and flea market combined.
- eBay also represents the products of several major U.S. brands, including General Motors.

eBay are now growing, which also has positive implications for the profitability of the business. eBay's revenue comes from two sources, the initial Insertion Fee, and an auctioneer's "cut" of the final sales value. The contract remains only between the buyer and seller. eBay acquired PayPal in 2002, for $1.5 billion in stock, and 20% of the company revenue now comes from this source.

E Eames Chairs

Originator: Charles Eames	MOMA One Man Show: 1946
Birthplace: St. Louis, MO	Eames Lounge Chair: 1956
Date of Birth: June 17, 1907	Aluminum Group Furniture: 1958
Office of Charles and Ray Eames:	Eames Chaise: 1968
Opened 1942	Today's Price: Eames Chaise $4,915

Charles Eames and his wife Ray were a significant force in the movement to modernize post–World War II America. Their exploration of new shapes and materials, and their understanding of mass production, enabled them to produce simple design classics that are still to be found in many homes and offices, and remain in production to this day. Eames studied architecture and design at Michigan's Cranbrook Academy of Art, and became head of the industrial design department there. His breakthrough to a wider audience came in 1940, when he won the "Organic Design" competition held by New York's Museum of Modern Art. The Eames moved to Los Angeles in 1941, where they built the famous Eames House (constructed from prefabricated industrial materials), and opened a design office in Venice, California. Their portfolio of fiberglass, plastic resin, and wire mesh chairs propelled the couple to celebrity status. They collaborated with the Federal Government to produce several items for the Armed Forces, including the Emeco 1006 aluminum chair for the Navy. Many of their designs are still available, having become an integral part of every day life and generic "good taste."

Did you know?
- When he and Ray moved to California, Eames's day job was as a set designer on *Mrs. Miniver*.
- Many people assumed that Ray was Eames's brother.

*"Design is the appropriate combination
of materials in order to solve a problem."*
Charles Eames

Edison Light Bulb

E

Birthplace: Menlo Park, NJ

Originator: Thomas Alva Edison

Date Introduced: December 1879

First Public Review: *New York Herald*,
   December 21, 1879

Company: Edison General Electric

First Residence Lit By Electricity: Sarah
   Jordan's boarding house

First Power Station: Pearl Street, Lower
   Manhattan, 1882

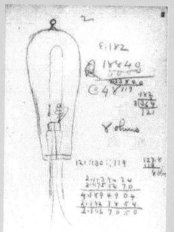

When Thomas Edison built his 100 feet by 25 feet laboratory in Menlo Park, New Jersey (in 1876), he called it his "invention factory." Within three years of occupancy, he had invented both the phonograph and the incandescent light bulb. One of the challenges he faced was in finding a suitable material for the bulb filament—and he experimented with such materials as carbonized threads, paper, and bamboo. The bulb itself was just part of his achievement. The real goal was to provide safe electrical circuits, switches, and adequate generating facilities. By 1882, these dreams were a reality culminating in the first commercial power station in Pearl Street, Manhattan. The company that Edison began eventually became General Electric; by that time, in true Edison style, he was on to something else.

Above: An early sketch of the light bulb.
Right: Edison's Menlo Park Laboratory in the late 1870s.
Far Right: Edison's Incandescent Lamp featured a carbonized paper filament and platinum screw clamps.

"The electric light has caused me the greatest amount of study and has required the most elaborate experiments."

Edison

Did you know?

- Edison patented more than 1,000 inventions in his life.
- His first attempt at a successful lamp used carbonized thread as a filament and burned for 13 hours.
- The first commercial use was on the ocean vessel *Columbia*, 1880.
- Edison gave potential employees a 150 question "mental fitness test."
- The famous Menlo Park laboratory was torn down but is shortly to be rebuilt as a memorial to Edison's work there.

E

Etch A Sketch

Birthplace: Ohio Art Company

Originator: Arthur Granjean

Hometown Now: Bryan, OH

Date Introduced: 1960

Today's Price: around $10

Number of Products: 10 plus

Number Sold: 100 million plus

Etch A Sketch Club: 2,000 members
plus

Member: National Toy Hall of Fame

The world's favorite drawing toy was conceived by French auto mechanic Arthur Granjean. Its white knobs have now been twiddled in over seventy countries, and Etch A Sketch is now available with Zooper sounds and color. The Ohio Art Company first saw the Granjean's "L'Ecran Magique" at the 1959 Nuremburg International Toy Fair. They decided to adopt the product, and paid $25,000 for the right to produce the newly renamed Etch A Sketch. The company began to market and advertise the product at once, and by Christmas 1960, it was one of the hottest toys in the U.S. The production lines were kept running on Christmas Eve to fulfil demand.

Although the company has offered various versions of the Etch A Sketch over the decades, the internal workings of the "Magic Screen" have remained virtually unchanged. The back of the screen is coated with a mixture of aluminum powder and plastic beads, which are scraped by the (knob-controlled) stylus to make a thin line.

The image is deleted by gentle shaking. The Etch A Sketch has launched many artistic careers and remains popular to this day. New versions of the Etch a Sketch include the Scribbler, Easter Egg, Love to, Pocket, Hot Pocket, Jelly Color Pocket, Electronic, Zooper Sounds, and Keychain. But the Classic hasn't changed at all, and is the iconic version that parents will recall.

"It is durable, fosters creativity, and has no pieces to lose. As a parent this is a near perfect toy."

Epinions

Did you know?

- The company celebrated its twenty-fifth anniversary with a silver Etch A Sketch. The knobs were encrusted with sapphires and blue topaz.
- A fully working keychain-size Etch A Sketch is now available ($5.99).
- The Etch A Sketch calendar featured scenes from the '60s drawn with the toy.

Fender Stratocaster

F

Birthplace: Fullerton, CA

Originator: Leo Fender

Hometown Now: Corona, CA

Date Introduced: 1954

Stratocaster vibrato patented: 1956

Original Price: $249.50

Today's Price: $499.99 upward

(U.S.-made Stratocasters)

Imported Models: From $150

Number Sold: 1,000,000+ worldwide

Instrument and amplifier designer Leo Fender (1909–1991) had already enjoyed substantial success with his solid-bodied Telecaster electric guitar at the start of the 1950s. Musicians visiting his factory in Fullerton, California, provided valuable feedback on the "Tele's" strengths and weaknesses, and their comments helped to shape the new, more versatile instrument, named the "Stratocaster," which Fender

*"I like to play all kinds of guitars ...
but I wasn't getting the sound I really
wanted until I got a Stratocaster."*
Mark Knopfler, *Guitar Player* magazine

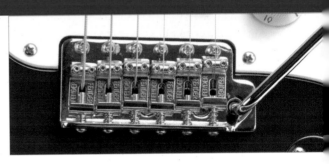

launched in 1954. It won further plaudits for the firm, and remains one of the most popular and influential of all guitars.

The Strat's three pickups (one more than the Tele) offer a choice of timbres, and its ingeniously simple vibrato is operated by pressing down an arm screwed into the bridge unit; this causes the bridge to pivot, slackening the string tension and producing a pitch bend. When the arm is released, a set of springs, anchored inside the body, return it to its normal position and bring the strings back to pitch. The Stratocaster's contoured body allows the instrument to rest snugly against a player's body—and even its jack socket receptacle is angled to reduce the fumble factor when plugging in an amplifier lead!

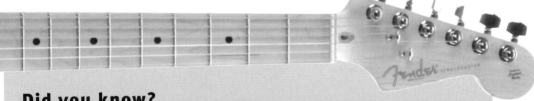

Did you know?

- Budget and mid-price versions of the Strat are manufactured in Asia and Mexico; premium models come from Fender's U.S. plant in Corona, CA.
- Though a brilliant designer, Leo Fender never learned to play guitar.
- Top Strat users include Jimi Hendrix and Buddy Holly.

Ferris Wheel

F

Birthplace: Chicago, IL

Originator: George Washington Gale
   Ferris Jr.

Date Introduced: 1893

Wheel Diameter: 250 feet

Wheel Circumference: 825 feet

Cost to Build: $380,000

Cost of Ride: $0.50

Revenue During World's Fair:
   $726,805.50

George Ferris was a Pittsburgh, Pennsylvania, bridge-builder who had begun his career in the railroad industry. Ferris founded his company, G.W.G. Ferris & Co., to explore the possibilities of structural steel. The organizers of the Chicago World's Fair of 1893 wanted to construct a giant wheel to rival the 984-foot Eiffel Tower of 1889. It was to commemorate the 400th anniversary of Columbus' landing in America. But by 1891, Daniel H. Burnham was complaining that the fair authorities had failed to find a design that "met the expectations of the people." His concern inspired Ferris, who immediately sketched a design on his dinner napkin. A contemporary described him as a "wild-eyed man with wheels in his head." Ferris inspired an entire generation of fairground attractions, which continue to thrill to this day.

Did you know?

- Ferris' wheel was transferred to St. Louis for the 1904 Exposition.
- The first wheel was dismantled in 1906, having been sold for scrap metal for $1,800.
- The "Wonder Wheel" was built at Coney Island in the early '20s.

Flintstones Vitamins

Flintstones Hometown: Bedrock, USA

Originators: William Hanna and Joseph Barbera

Date Introduced: 1968

Flavors: 7 including chocolate

Character Shapes: 10

Today's Price: Flintstones Children's Complete from $7.39

Manufacturer: Bayer

Bayer Headquarters: Morristown, NJ

ABC first broadcast *The Flintstones* on **September 30, 1960. The cartoon became the first and longest running situation comedy shown on prime-time television.** The show helped to establish Hanna-Barbera Productions as a major Hollywood animation studio and launched a multi-million dollar merchandising business. Chewable Flintstones vitamins are probably the most enduring of products endorsed by the show's endearing characters, although Fruity and Cocoa Pebbles breakfast cereals

Did you know?

- Flintstones vitamins are available for children from the age of two.
- The tablets contain vitamins A, B, C, D, E, calcium, and phosphorus for long-term growth and development.
- Betty Rubble was added in 1995, when the Flintstones' car was discontinued.

are also still popular. The vitamins also sponsored the show for several seasons. The six different formulas are made in the shapes of eight characters – Fred, Wilma, Pebbles, Bamm-Bamm, Dino, Barney, Betty, and Great Gazoo. Specific Flintstones formulas are available for kids that don't eat enough of specific food groups such as fruit, vegetables, meat, and fish—or are simply fussy eaters.

Ford Model T

F

Birthplace: Detroit, MI

Originator: Henry Ford

Hometown Now: Dearborn, MI

Date Introduced: 1908

Spokesperson: Henry Ford

Original Price: $825

Today's Price: $21,000

Models available in 1908: 5

Number Sold in 1908: 10,660

Stock Exchange Symbol: F

The best known automobile manufacturer of all time was forty years old when his first real mass production car, the Model A, was born in 1903. Henry Ford's previous career had been precarious, to say the least. Early backers were disenchanted with his fixation on racing projects, and they deserted him en masse to support Henry Leland, the founder of Cadillac. Despite this, his 999 was the first car to circle Michigan's celebrated Grosse Pointe track in less than a minute in 1901.

Ford finally buckled down to true mass production, and within five years, he had launched one of his greatest automobiles, the iconic Model T. Introduced in the fall of 1908, the "Tin Lizzie" (as the car became affectionately known) was put on sale for just $825. Its simple suspension system utilized two transverse leaf springs. Its chassis and engine components were made from vanadium steel—a light, durable material developed by Childe Harold Wills, Ford's chief engineer and factory manager. Another innovation lay in the design of its large rear wheels, which gave the powertrain extra grip. And for the first time, a wide range of factory-fitted options were available to Ford customers, making it possible for each T to be equipped for an individual's needs. The vehicle's affordability and availability were to change the American way of life forever.

Did you know?

- The Ford Motor Company was incorporated on June 16, 1903, with capital of $28,000. Ford owned 25.5% of the business.
- The Model T stayed in production for two decades and sold over 15 million.
- Henry Ford's obituary read "The Father of the Automobile Dies."

"We use transverse springs for the same reason that we use round wheels—because we have found nothing better for the purpose."
Henry Ford

Ford Boss 429 Mustang

F

Birthplace: Detroit, MI

Originator: Lee Iacocca

Hometown Now: Dearborn, MI

Date Introduced: 1964

  (Boss 429 Introduced: 1969)

Original Price: $4,932

Today's Price: $64,000

Brake hp: 375@5600rpm

Number Sold: 857

Stock Exchange Symbol: F

Ford introduced the Mustang in 1964, under the auspices of Lee Iacocca and the Ford Studio team. The car was Ford's response to the improving economy of the early '60s, when consumers were looking for smaller cars equipped with luxury and good performance. A million examples were sold in its first two years of introduction, and the Mustang remains in production to this day.

The Boss 429 was based on the Sportsroof Mustang, but featured Ford's "Shotgun" 429-ci engine—intended for NASCAR racing and included on this car to accord with a NASCAR rule stating that engines used on the track should also be fitted to at least 500 production models. The 429 Mustangs were built at Kar-Kraft in Brighton, Michigan,

"Mustangs, like hamburgers, have become an American institution."

Car Life magazine

where the Sportsroof design underwent extensive modifications, enabling it to accept a larger engine block and giving it a beefed-up suspension. The cars retained the interior styling and basic outside appearance of the Sportsroof Mustang, but could cover a quarter mile in 14 seconds and accelerate from 0–60 mph in 7.1 seconds. Following the launch of the first Bosses by Kar-Kraft in January 1969, reactions were very mixed. *Car Life* magazine rated the vehicle as "the best enthusiast car Ford has ever produced." However, others castigated its performance – designer Larry Shinoda described it as a "slug in the Mustang" – and the model remained in production for only two years, the final car leaving Kar-Kraft in January 1970.

Did you know?

- *Playboy* had several '69 Mustangs sprayed "Playboy Pink" to promote the magazine. Ford subsequently adopted the color, and these cars are now highly collectible.
- Lee Iacocca became known as "The Father of the Mustang."
- An entire generation was named after the car–the "Mustang Generation."

F   Formica

Birthplace: Pittsburgh, PA

Originator: Daniel J. O'Connor

Employed By: Westinghouse

Product Developed: 1912

Patent Filed: 1913

Formica Company Established: 1913

Original Capital: $7,500

Formica Hometown Now: Cincinnati, OH

Number Of Products: 400 plus

Company Name: Formica Corporation

Formica was developed to cater for the improved insulating materials required by the new industrial age of the twentieth century. Daniel J. O'Connor, a young scientist, had the idea of coating fabric with resin and curing it to form a light, tough laminated plastic. The product was the substitute "for mica," the previous form of electrical insulation. The next major development for the company came when they worked out how to print sheets of the material, to make hardworking, decorative finishes. A million lunch counters were born.

Did you know?

- Formica is the world's leading name in decorative surfaces.
- Formica is one of the world's 10 best-known brand names.
- The material has undergone a huge surge in popularity over the last decade.

Frigidaire

Birthplace: Fort Wayne, IN

Originator: Alfred Mellowes

Hometown now: Martinez, GA

Date Introduced: 1916

Original Price: $395 (in the 1920s)

Today's Price: Mid-range model $529

Number of Products: 46 plus refrigerators

Number Sold: 50 million by 1965

There was a long history of attempts to cool food mechanically. However, the first "self-contained" fridge (as we know it today) was manufactured by Alfred Mellowes in his backyard washhouse. It was manufactured by the Guardian Refrigerator Company, which was purchased by General Motors in 1919. Quickly, they re-named the company "Frigidaire." As well as automotive-style mass production, the acquisition brought development capital into the business. The first all-steel cabinet was introduced in 1926.

Did you know?

- The refrigerator is America's most popular domestic appliance and 99.5% of homes have one.
- Frigidaire, now part of Electrolux, continues to produces fridges. Its slogan "Built for Generations" is literally true.

F Frisbee

Birthplace: San Luis Obispo, CA

Originators: Fred Morrison and
   Warren Franscioni

Hometown Now: Emeryville, CA

"Frisbee" Named: 1958

First Mass Produced: 1957

Today's Price: From $9.99

Number of Products: 9 disc types

Number Sold: 200 million plus

Stock Exchange Symbol: MAT

During the 1870s, the Frisbie Baking Company of
Bridgeport, Connecticut, began using thin
metal bases for their pies; these tins became
playthings for college kids, who enjoyed tossing them
through the air. In 1948, a plastic disc based on the
pie-plate shape and christened the "Flyin' Saucer"
was developed by two Air Force veterans, Fred
Morrison and Warren Franscioni, in San Luis Obispo,
California. The toy (owned since 1957 by Wham-O
based in nearby San Gabriel) was re-named the
"Frisbee," and went on to sell over 100 million items.
In 1994, Mattel bought the brand.

Did you know?

- The Frisbee's predecessors
  were named "Flyin'
  Saucer" and "Pluto
  Platter" to cash in on the
  UFO mania sweeping
  America in the late '40s
  and '50s.

George Foreman Grill

Birthplace: Mt. Prospect, IL

Originator: Salton

Hometown now: Lake Forest, IL

Date Introduced: 1994

Spokesperson: George Foreman

Foreman Website: BigGeorge.com

Today's Price: $19.99 plus

Number of Products: around 45

Number Sold: 40 million plus

Stock Exchange Symbol: SFP

Did you know?

- The Salton brand name was introduced in 1947.
- The George Foreman grill virtually created the concept of electric grilling.
- Propane-powered outdoor George Foreman grills were launched in 2001.

George Foreman's ringing endorsement of the Salton company's range of cooking appliances bearing his name has been good news for both parties. The Illinois-based firm's imported, fat-reducing grills seemed unlikely to become successful when they were first shown at a trade fair in 1994; but the Texan ex-boxing champion—once known for his surliness and short temper, but now an affable family man, Baptist minister, and dedicated fund raiser for good causes—was eager to find suitable products to promote. The two parties came together the following year, and, after a sluggish start, an inspired series of ad campaigns began convincing million of customers to purchase the "lean, mean, fat-reducing grilling machine" that Foreman "was so proud of, he put his name on." So far, more than 40 million of the grills have been sold, and in 1999, Salton, which had been giving Foreman a set percentage of its profits, acquired permanent rights to use his name on the product line, paying him $127.5 million in cash and $10 million in company stock.

G

Gary Fisher Mountain Bikes

Birthplace: San Anselmo, CA

Originator: Gary Fisher

Hometown Now: Waterloo, WI

Date Introduced: 1974

Spokesperson: *Smithsonian* magazine

Original Price: $1320

Today's Price: $3299.99

Number of Models in Range: 52

Term "Mountain Bike" Invented: 1979
  by Charlie Kelly

It all began when 12-year-old Gary Fisher began competitive riding on road and track in 1963. Just 11 years later, he started to build his first prototype mountain bike—the famous "Klunker." This machine used motorcycle brakes, a '30s-era frame, and a wide gear range to tackle all terrains. In 1979, Gary and partner Charlie Kelly released the first batch of 160 refined Klunker-style mountain bikes to an eager market. Their bike range has always seemed deeply cool, with hip names like Cake, Sugar, Wahoo, Ziggurat, Hoo Koo E Koo, and X-Caliber. Names given to bikes that were as innovative as they sounded.

The 1987 Procaliber was rated one of the Top Ten Best mountain bikes of all time. As a competitor, Gary weaves his practical experience into the development of his bikes. He describes himself as, "still riding and racing, listening and learning" and this

Did you know?

- In 1968, Gary Fisher was banned from competitive racing for having long hair.
- By 1972, long hair was OK, so he was allowed back on the circuit.
- Gary has been inducted into the Mountain Bike Hall of Fame.
- The first full suspension bike was prototyped in 1990.
- Gary Fisher Bikes has been owned by Trek Bicycles since 1993.

"*The Founding Father of Mountain Bikes.*"
Smithsonian magazine

spirit continues to drive the company forward. In 2002 he launched the first
production 29-inch wheel mountain bike, The Two-Niner. Larger wheels give the bike
a capability to go "faster and further." We feature the Cake, part of the current Gary
Fisher range.

G   G.I. Joe

Birthplace: Pawtucket, RI

Originator: Don Levine

Position: Creative Director Hasbro

Hometown Now: Pawtucket, RI

Date Introduced: 1964

"Vintage" Joe Discontinued: 1976

"Real American Hero" Launched: 1982

Stock Exchange Symbol: HAS

Parent Company: Hassenfeld Bros./Hasbro

Toy merchandiser Stan Weston brought the G.I. Joe concept "a rugged-looking scale doll for boys" to Don Levine, Hasbro's creative director, in 1964. Weston had been inspired by the TV series *The Lieutenant*. Levine quickly realized the potential of a toy for boys that would have limitless accessories, and decided to go ahead with G.I. Joe. From the beginning, Hasbro has been careful to market the toy as an action figure, not a doll. The granddaddy of all action figures was launched later in the year, with a huge selection of 75 figures, vehicles, uniforms, and accessories. The line-up included the "G.I. Nurse," who is now worth in excess of $6,000. G.I. Joe was soon to become the single greatest character brand in boys' toys and has been reincarnated more than a dozen times. Sales ran into trouble in the post-Vietnam era and Hasbro was forced to re-invent the soldier as an adventurer to reflect the change in world politics. G.I. Joe was withdrawn between 1976 and 1982. The figure also shrank (to 8 inches in 1977), shrank again (to 3 inches in 1982), grew again (to 12 inches in 1992), and shrank again (to 4 and 6 inches in 1995 and 1996). Hasbro plans to launch a completely new figure in fall 2005, supported for the first time by a dedicated TV series.

"*For a long time during my early childhood, the only thing I wanted at Christmas was G.I. Joe.*"

The Beachhead, a website dedicated to G.I. Joe

NOTE: Adult should remove and discard plastic fasteners.

Did you know?

• G.I. Joe was inducted into the National Toy Hall of Fame in November 2004.

• G.I. Joe is now starring in the movie *Valor vs. Venom*.

• Hasbro also owns Mr. Potato Head, Tonka trucks, and Monopoly.

G

Gillette Razor

Birthplace: Boston, MA

Originator: King Camp Gillette (concept) and William Nickerson (technology)

Hometown now: Boston, MA

Date Introduced: 1903

Original Price: $0.05 per blade

Number of Products: 14 blade and razor ranges for men and women

Stock Exchange Symbol: G

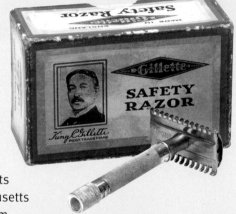

King Camp Gillette (1855–1932) was a salesman in search of a product. He conceived the idea of a razor with a disposable blade one morning in 1895, having been irritated to discover that his own shaving tackle had lost its edge. Realizing that replaceable blades would be highly convenient, and that there would be a perpetual demand for them, he set about discovering how to produce them easily and cheaply. A method of cutting blades from sheets of pressed steel was developed by a Massachusetts Institute of Technology–trained chemist, William Nickerson, and the first razors went on sale in 1903. Early sales were disappointing, but demand soon rose and within a few years, the Gillette Company was making hundreds of thousands of razors and millions of blades. According to *Fortune* magazine, "Gillette still sells five times as many razor blades as anyone else."

Did you know?

- "There is no other article for individual use so universally known or widely distributed."—King Camp Gillette
- Gillette was bought by Procter & Gamble for $57 billion in January 2005.
- 63% of Gillette's profit is still derived from the sale of blades and razors.

Goodyear Tires

Birthplace: Springfield, MA

Originator: Charles Goodyear

Hometown Now: Akron, OH

Date Introduced: (patent for vulcanized
   rubber) 1844

First Pneumatic Tire: 1888 (Dunlop)

First Tubeless Tire: 1903 (Goodyear)

Today's Price: $193.95 (Eagle LS
   Performance tire)

Number Sold: 150 million plus

Charles Goodyear (1800–1860) was the inventor of vulcanized rubber, the first and most versatile of the modern plastics. After years of privation and spells in debtors' prison, Goodyear finally managed to formulate hardened rubber in 1839. This discovery facilitated the introduction of Dunlop's very first pneumatic bicycle tires, the forerunner of Goodyear's huge global business. To this day, tire sales account for 82% of the company revenues, and the company manufactures tires of every kind, for passenger and racing cars (NASCAR and Formula One), planes, and trucks. But poor Charles died before Goodyear was founded (1898), in $200,000 of debt.

Did you know?

- Charles Goodyear was a life-long socialist. He said that "Life should not be estimated exclusively by the standard of dollars and cents."
- When the Goodyear family was destitute, Charles made a rubber dinner service.
- Goodyear had sales of $4.7 billion in the first quarter of 2005.

G Google

Birthplace: Stanford, CA

Originators: Larry Page and
   Sergey Brin

Hometown Now: Mountain View, CA

Date Introduced: 1998

Original Name: BackRub

Members in 2002: 34 million

Revenue First Quarter 2005: $1.256
   billion

Stock Exchange Symbol: GOOG (NASDA

Larry Page and Sergey Brin were impoverished computer science students at Stanford University, who dreamt of a search engine that would organize the burgeoning content of the web. Friend and founder of Yahoo! David Filo, was encouraging and recommended that they should start a company to develop their ideas. The pair had financed a terabyte of memory by maxing out their credit cards, and

iMac

Did you know?

- "Google" comes from "googol," a word coined by Milton Sirotta to mean the numeral 1 followed by 100 zeroes.
- Google's mission is to organize the world's information.
- Google aspires to be the ultimate "answer machine."

desperately needed investment. Andy Bechtolsheim (the cofounder of Sun Microsystems) gave them a check for $100,000, and Google Inc. was born. Page and Brin started the company with $1,000,000, three employees (including themselves) and a table tennis table for their board meetings. A far cry from today's famously worker-friendly "Googleplex," with its healthy restaurants, massage room, and baby grand piano.

Green Bay Packers

Birthplace: Green Bay, WI

Originators: Curly Lambeau and
    George Calhoun

Date Established: 1919

Home Stadium: Lambeau Field

Dedicated: September 29, 1957

Capacity: 72,601

Original Stadium Cost: $960,000

Owner: Public nonprofit corporation

Number of Stockholders: 111,507

When Curly Lambeau and George Calhoun decided to put their football team together, they approached Curly's employer, the Indian Packing Company (where he earned $250 per month working as a clerk), to sponsor the team sweaters. A legend was born. The "Packers" were immediately successful, winning 10 games and losing just 1 in their first season. These early games were played in an open field. But the team outplayed its humble origins to win more championships (12) than any other team in pro football and reach national NFL stature.

Did you know?

- The Packers won the first of three straight national professional football championships in 1929.
- The Packers were the first professional football team to have their own Hall of Fame.
- To watch Packer games in absolute luxury, you can rent one of 14 Super Boxes at $115,000 per season.

G Greyhound Bus

Birthplace: Hibbing MN

Originators: Raymond Loewy/
   General Motors

Hometown Now: Naperville, IL

Date Introduced: 1954

Retired from Service: 1978

Scenicruisers Built: 1,001

Manufacturing Plant: Pontiac, MI

Today's Sales: $4.63 billion

Stock Exchange Symbol: LI

Greyhound was established in Hibbing, Minnesota in 1914. The company grew quickly in the 1920s and rival companies were encouraged by the Interstate Commerce Commission to ensure that Greyhound didn't become a monopoly. However by the time that the Interstate Highways began to cross the country in the 1950s, private car ownership was seriously challenging public transportation. Greyhound produced one of their most favored buses, the Scenicruiser, at this time. Designed by Raymond Loewy, the first celebrity industrial designer, and built by General Motors, the bus was an exclusive Greyhound model and had wonderful streamline styling. Suspended on air rather than the old-style metal springs the bus reached new standards of riding comfort. It offered accommodation on two levels, ten passengers were seated forward with the driver and 33 more in the raised observation level. It featured air-conditioning and ventilation systems, which kept the coach cool during the summer and delightfully warm in winter. The bus took ten years to develop.

Although movies like *Midnight Cowboy* portrayed Greyhound travel as cool, the heyday of long distance public travel by bus was probably over by the '60s. Despite this, the company survived through 30 years of independence until being acquired by Laidlaw Inc. in 1998. The company reemerged as Laidlaw International in 2003. Laidlaw is still proud to operate it's Greyhound division, concentrating on charter and sightseeing services.

> *"The driver has every reason to take pride in the Scenicruiser - a pride that is shared by all Greyhound employees, it's stockholders, and it's management"*
>
> Orville S. Caeser, President, Greyhound Lines

Did you know?

- The bus had two engines so that if one broke down it could return to the depot on the other.
- The lavatory had a special high speed exhaust fan when the door was locked from the inside – just like a passenger airliner.
- Raymond Loewy also designed the slenderized coke bottle, another American Icon! (See pages 74-75.)

G

Grocery Cart

Birthplace: Oklahoma City, OK

Originator: Sylvan Nathan Goldman

Date Introduced: Patented 1938

Today's Price: $75–$115 depending upon size

Life of carts kept indoors: 10 years

Life of carts kept outside: 5 years

Carts in use today: 25 million

Slogan: "Everybody's using them, why not you?" (Goldman)

Sylvan Goldman owed a chain of Oklahoma grocery stores called Standard/Piggly-Wiggly, and was frustrated that shoppers finished when their hand baskets were full. He came up with the concept of mounting two baskets, and wheels on a folding chair to make the first grocery cart. He and mechanic Fred Young refined the design, and established the Folding Carrier Company. By 1940, the grocery cart was so intrinsic to American life that it appeared on the cover of *The Saturday Evening Post*. The telescoping, or nesting, cart was invented by Orla Watson, which meant that the carts folded into one another for storage. The first was used at Floyd Day's Super Market in 1947. Smart shopping carts with interactive screens are now on their way to a grocery store near you.

Did you know?
- Shoppers were initially reluctant to use grocery carts. Men thought that they made them look weak, while women thought they were unfashionable.
- Cartless retailers have suffered a sales slowdown in recent years, whereas sales are booming for those that use carts.

Hallmark Cards

Birthplace: Kansas City, MO

Originator: Joyce Clyde Hall

Hometown now: Kansas City, MO

Date Introduced: 1910

Number Sold: 3 billion annually

Share of Greeting Card Market:
 50 percent

Most Popular Occasion to Send a Card:
 High school graduation

U.S. retail outlets: 44,000

The story of the Hallmark Company is a classic American tale of rags to riches. Joyce Clyde Hall arrived in Kansas with hardly any money at all, but used what he had to start a tiny business printing postcards. Soon, he realised the potential for high-quality greetings cards sold with an envelope, and began making Valentine and Christmas cards in 1915. The company continued to innovate, and introduced the first dedicated gift-wrap in 1917. J. C. Hall and his brother started using the "Hallmark"

brand in 1928. They felt that it exuded the "quality" image they wanted to present, as well as encapsulating the family name. They also originated one of the most famous tag lines ever—"When you care enough to send the very best."

Did you know?

- 20 percent of the Company is owned by the "Hallmarkers" the company employees.
- There really is a Hallmark card for every occasion: losing a tooth, successful potty training, having triplets, and becoming a grandmother.

Hammond Organ

H

Birthplace: Radio City, NY

Originator: Laurens Hammond

Hometown Now: Addison, IL

Date Introduced: 1935

1935 Production: 2,500 organs

1959 Net Worth: $17,044,000

Original Price: $1,250

Today's Price: XK-3 $2,195

Company Publication: The *Hammond Times*

Laurens Hammond was an extraordinarily ingenious man who invented and perfected many products, including the automatic bridge table (selling 14,000 at $25) and 3-D glasses. Although he was no musician himself, his desire to bring music into the homes of the masses led him to devise his Hammond organ in the early '30s. The "Model A" was unveiled at Radio City's RCA Building in 1935, to great critical acclaim. Hammond ran the company until 1955 and instigated a program of continual technical improvement. He continued inventing until his death in 1973, by which time he held 110 electrical and mechanical patents.

Did you know?

- Laurens' father, William Hammond, committed suicide when his Chicago-based bank failed in 1897.
- Henry Ford and George Gershwin both placed preproduction orders in 1934.
- President Roosevelt was presented with a Hammond in 1940.

Harlem Globetrotters

Birthplace: Chicago, IL

Originator: Coach Abe Saperstein

Hometown Now: Phoenix, AZ

Team Founded: 1926

Original Name: Savoy Big Five

20,000th Career Game: 1998

Replica Globetrotter Jersey: $60

Team Sponsor: Burger King (since 2002)

2004 Tour Attendance: 1.3 million

Owner & Chairman: Mannie Jackson

Abe Saperstein originally formed the team in 1926 to promote Chicago's Savoy Ballroom, but their basketball skills failed to boost attendance. So, the team went out on the road to survive. Their wandering tradition had begun. They took on all comers, and lived a punishing schedule. In 1930, Saperstein changed the team name to the Harlem New York Globetrotters to emphasize its African-American heritage. Their playing circuit gradually expanded until 1947, when the Globetrotters played their first overseas game in Hawaii. Since then, they have become a truly international phenomenon, playing in more than 117 countries, including Africa and China. Mannie Jackson acquired the team in 1993 and became the first black owner of a major national team. The Globetrotters fantastic commercial success dates from this time, and the fan base is bigger than ever.

Did you know?

- Inman Jackson became the team's first "Clown Prince" in 1939.
- Pope John XXIII granted the Globetrotters an audience in 1959.

H Harley-Davidson Fat Boy

Birthplace: Milwaukee, WI

Originator: Willie G

Hometown Now: Milwaukee, WI

Date Introduced: 1990

Spokesperson: Clement Salvadori, Road Scholar

Today's Price: FLSTFI from $16,845

Stock Exchange Symbol: HDI

By the mid-1980s, the company that Bill Harley and Art Davidson had started in 1903 was the only survivor of more than 300 motorcycle manufacturers founded before World War I. Mounting competition from Japan threatened and the company was all too aware of the need to modernize its operation in order to keep up. But while there was a need for technical progress, it was Harley-Davidson's strong retro styling–hinting at design clues from the '40s through the '60s–that was paramount to its image. In turn, this engendered a strong sense of patriotic buying fervor in the motorcycling public. This trend repeated itself a full ten years later in the automobile market, with cars such as the Mustang returning to their stylistic roots, but H-D led the way. The motorcycle that so successfully combined elements of the past and present– in an eye-catching package–was aptly named the "Fat Boy." In essence, it was a development of the "Softail," but sported chromed disc wheels, chunky flared mudguards, mammoth light and nacelle, and bulbous shotgun pipes. The paint job is delightfully muted in Silver or Black.

Specifications: 15th Anniversary Limited Edition Fat Boy

Engine: Twin Cam 88B

Displacement: 95 cubic inches

Bore and Stroke: 3.87x4 inches

Compression Ratio: 9.4:1

Torque: 73 ft-lbs at 4,250 rpm

"As long as Americans have money Harley-Davidson will succeed."
Clement Salvadori, Road Scholar

Fuel System: Electronic Sequential
   Port Fuel Injection
Transmission: 5-speed
Frame: Steel, double downtube
Suspension: F. Telescopic Fork;
   R. Shocks
Brakes: F&R Disc

Wheelbase: 64.5 inches
Weight: 675 pounds
Fuel Capacity: 5 gallons
Oil Capacity: 3.5 quarts
Tires: F. MT90B16 72H, R. 150/
   80B16 71H
Top Speed: 119 mph

H Heinz Ketchup

Birthplace: Pittsburgh, PA

Originator: Henry J. Heinz

Heinz Headquarters: Pittsburgh, PA

Date Introduced: 1876

Today's Price: $1.55 (14 fl oz)

Ketchup Varieties: Easy Squeeze, One Carb, Light, No Salt Added, Organic, Hot & Spicy

Number Sold: 1 billion annually

In 1869, Henry John Heinz (1844-1919) and a neighbor from his hometown of Pittsburgh, L. Clarence Noble, launched a food-manufacturing partnership. Their firm went bankrupt in 1875, but Heinz was soon back in business with a new company, and a new product: tomato ketchup, supplied in transparent bottles so customers could see the contents' quality and purity for themselves. Only a few decades earlier, tomatoes had been an object of suspicion to many Americans: in 1820, tomato grower Colonel Robert Gibbon Johnson had resorted to standing on the steps of a New England courthouse and eating a sample of his crop to prove its wholesomeness. However, by the 1870s, there was a growing demand for the vegetable, and Heinz's thick, flavorsome concoction was an immediate success. Its popularity secured the future of H.J. Heinz and Co., which has gone on to be a world leader in the food industry.

Did you know?

- There were never "57 varieties" of Heinz products; founder H.J. Heinz chose the number because he thought it looked intriguing.
- Heinz paid $57 million to have the new home of the Pittsburgh Steelers named Heinz Field.

Hershey Bar

Birthplace: Lancaster, PA

Originator: Milton S. Hershey

Hometown Now: Hershey, PA

Date Introduced: 1900

Annual Sales: $4 billion plus

Percentage of US Chocolate
 Business: 95%

Number of Products: 7 varieties plus

Nutritional Information: 43g bar,
 230 calories

Milton S. Hershey was a candy **manufacturer who made a conscious decision to bring chocolate within the reach of the ordinary American.** At the time, it was very much a confectionary for the rich, but Hershey's mass production techniques made the sweet treat universally available. He built his factory in the heart of the Pennsylvania dairy country, and gradually built up the business by adding more product lines.

Did you know?

- The streets of Hershey, PA are lined with Hershey Kisses-shaped streetlights.
- Milton Hershey was so devoted to his wife, Catherine, that he brought her fresh flowers every day of their marriage.
- Milton was a great philanthropist, and endowed many institutions.

Milk chocolate with almonds was brought out in 1905, and the well loved "Kiss" in 1907. Hershey's moderately priced chocolate retained its popularity even during the Great Depression, so that no Hershey workers were laid off. The company is now a confectionary giant, and owns many of the most familiar American brands, including Reese's and Kit Kat, but the business still remains a strong supporter of non-profit organizations.

Hobie Surfboard

Birthplace: Laguna Beach, CA

Originator: Hobart Alter Jr.

Hometown Now: San Juan Capistrano, CA

Date Introduced: 1950

Spokesperson: Hobie

Original Investment: $12,000

Today's Price: c. $633

Number of Products: 31 surfboard
   models plus

Number Sold: 250 per week in the '60s

When Hobart Alter Jr.'s father backed his Buick out of the garage to give his son room to work on his surfboards, he little thought that Hobie would become the most successful entrepreneur in surfing history. Still in high school, Hobie worked on his balsa wood boards for several years until he developed a technique of making boards out of polyurethane foam. He opened his shop, "Hobie Surfboards" in 1954, selling surfboards, skateboards, and apparel. In fact, Hobie invented many of the most innovative, affordable, and highest quality water sports products on the market today, including kayaks, and the Hobie 14 Catamaran. 100,000 of his boats are now sailing around the world. Hobie boards still carry the most evocative names, the Endless Summer, Retro Egg, and Day Glow Twin.

Did you know?

- Hobie's personal credo was, never to live East of the Pacific Coast Highway, or wear hard soled shoes.
- Hobie lived the California Endless Summer dream of the Beach Boys for real, and virtually invented surf culture.
- Hobie described his 1952 trip to Hawaii as the "best times of my life."

"The World is a Water Park, And Since 1950 We've Made The Best Rides."

Hobie

H Hollywood

Birthplace: Mount Lee,
   Hollywood Hills, CA

Originator: Hollywoodland
   Real Estate Group

Hometown Now: Mount Lee, CA

Date Introduced: 1923

Original Cost: $ 21,000

Length: 450 feet

Height: 45 feet

Weight: 450,000 lbs

The **HOLLYWOOD sign is one of the world's most evocative symbols — a metaphor for success, ambition, and glamour.** The original sign was built in 1923 at a cost of $21,000 as an advertisement for the Hollywoodland Real Estate Group and was originally lit by over 4,000 light bulbs. But by 1945, it had fallen into disrepair. The letter "H" toppled over in the wind. Restoration began in the '70s, with *Playboy* magnate Hugh Hefner raising the necessary funds, persuading various stars to adopt a letter each.

Did you know?

- Peg Entwhistle, a struggling 24- year-old actress jumped to her death from the top of "H" in 1932.
- The sign has been vandalized to read HOLLYWEED (to celebrate the drug culture), and HOLYWOOD (during the Pope's visit).
- The sign is Los Angeles Cultural-Historical Monument #111.

Hoover Vacuum Cleaner

Birthplace: Canton, OH

Originator: Murray Spangler

Hometown Now: Canton, OH

Commentator: Linda Cobb "The Queen of Clean"

Date Introduced: 1908

Today's Price: From $79.99

Number of Products: 70 plus

Number Sold: Leading brand

Stock Exchange Symbol: MYG

Murray Spangler was an inventor who supported himself with an evening job as a janitor. But dust from sweeping aggravated his asthma, so he assembled the world's first "suction sweeper" from a soapbox, fan, pillowcase, and broom handle. Spangler immediately recognized the commercial potential of his invention and started looking for investors. He gave the machine to family friend, Susan Hoover, to try in her home. She sang the praises of the machine to her husband, leather manufacturer W. H. "Boss" Hoover, and the rest, as they say, is history. Originally sold door-to-door with a free 10-day trial, Hoovers remain the industry leader to this day. Like many American successes, Hoover has always recognized the importance of advertising and marketing.

Did you know?

- Hoover remained family-owned until the early '40s, and is now a division of the Maytag Corporation.
  - The beater bar was introduced in 1926, "It beats as it sweeps as it cleans."
    - Hoover has its own baseball club, the "Hoover Sweepers." The team plays in 1860s costume.

Hot Wheels

Originator: Elliot Handler

Hometown Now: El Segundo, CA

Date Introduced: 1968

Hot Wheel Scale: 1/64th to 1/18th

Most Prolific Year: 2003 (706 models)

Most Common Casting: '57 Chevy

Today's Price: $19.99 (20-car pack)

Annual Revenue: $ 5.5 billion

Number Sold: 2 billion to 1998

Stock Exchange Symbol: MAT

Breakthrough products like Hot Wheels have made Mattel the world's largest toy company. Before these dynamite little cars were introduced in 1968, die-cast models were aimed at adults rather than children—they were for display, not play. The first 18 Hot Wheels models changed all that. At 2 inches long, they were designed to race on their unique orange plastic track, and built for power and performance. Their motive power came from gravity alone, but they were incredibly fast. The cars were immediately popular, and some Hot Wheels aficionados consider the first four years of production as a golden era. One hundred and eighteen castings were produced during this period, and some totally innovative features, including Specterflame paint colors and Redline tires were introduced. But Mattel has continued to develop the brand for over 35 years. The Hot Wheels line-up for 2005 included the Incredible Crash Dummies, Formula Fuelers, and AcceleRacers. There is also a huge Hot Wheels collectors market for vintage cars, some of which change hands for serious money. Hot Wheels is now a huge global brand in its own right, and Mattel estimates that at least 41 million children (mostly boys) have grown up playing with the little cars.

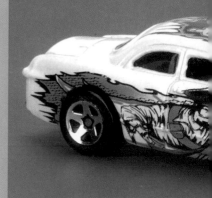

> *"35 Years of Speed, Power,
> Performance and Attitude."*
> Randy Leffingwell, author of *Hot Wheels*

Did you know?

- The average Hot Wheels collector has 1,155 cars.
- The average American child has 41 Hot Wheels cars.
- Mattel has now produced more cars than Detroit's Big Three manufacturers combined.
- Some Hot Wheels sets included a Supercharger.
- Accessories, including lap counters and speedometers, were available.
- "Sizzlers" had tiny battery-powered motors.
- "Fat Track" was black, rather than the usual orange.

Howard Johnson

Birthplace: Wollaston, MA	**Number of Howard Johnson Hotels:** 5(plus
Originator: Howard Dearing Johnson	
Hometown Now: New York, NY	**Annual Number of Guests:** 15,000,00(
Date Introduced: 1925	**Cendant CEO:** Henry R. Silverman
Locations: Canada to China	**Stock Exchange Symbol:** CD

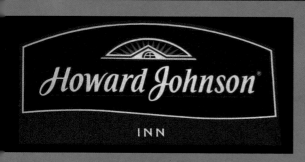

Howard Johnson started his business empire the hard way, burdened by his dead father's debts. But Johnson had a brilliant marketing mind and invented many retail concepts that we take for granted today. These include franchising, premium ice cream, "theme" restaurants, turnpike restaurants, and "Kids-Go-Free." He started out in 1925, when he borrowed $2,000 to buy a small corner drugstore in Wollaston, Massachusetts. He soon realized that his most popular line was ice cream, and he introduced "secret formula" flavors based on his mother's recipes. The enormous success of his ice creams led him to open beachfront ice cream stands, which were hugely profitable. This, in turn, resulted in the establishment of a roadside restaurant chain. He had

Did you know?

- The Howard Johnson restaurant chain contracted from 200 outlets to 12 in the early '40s, a victim of wartime gas rationing.
- At the company's peak in 1975, Howard Johnson had over 1,000 restaurants and 500 motor lodges.
- Howard Johnson died in 1972 at the age of 75.

> *"We've got a great name to live up to."*
> Howard Johnson TV commercial

107 restaurants by 1939 (with revenues of $10.5 million), stimulated by the growth of the U.S. highway system, and these became know as the "Host of the Highway." The *Howard Johnson Bible* set out high standards for franchise restaurants. In the '50s, the familiarity of the brand rivalled that of Coca-Cola, and its strength led to the launch of the Howard Johnson chain of motor lodges. There were over 500 of these by 1975. Difficult times were

to follow, with devastating competition from fast food restaurants and new hotel chains (Holiday Inn, Ramada, and Marriott). Cendant, the world's biggest lodging franchisor, now owns Howard Johnson. Its revenues and reputation are being restored, with the introduction of many new concepts, such as the Home Office Room and Kids Go HoJo.

133

Hula Hoop

H

Birthplace: Los Angeles, CA

Originators: Richard P. Knerr and
   Arthur "Spud" Melin

Hometown Now: Emeryville, CA

Date Introduced: 1958

Original Price: $1.98

Number of Products: 3 swirly colors,
   3 hoop sizes

Number Sold: 25 million in the first
   4 months

The Hula Hoop is an ancient invention—Egyptian children were spinning large hoops of dried grapevine on their hips three thousand years ago. Hoops were also made from wood, metal, and stiff grasses. But the inventors of the modern plastic version are Richard Knerr and Arthur Melin, the co-founders of Wham-O Inc. The company was also behind the modern revival of the Frisbee. Back in the '50s, Knerr and Melin heard from a visiting Australian that children in his country spun hoops made from bamboo around their waist. Knerr and Melin immediately thought of how they could make a commercial plastic version of the classic toy. They used the new material, Marlex, and launched the toy in a variety of hot colors. It was an instant success, and 25 million were sold in the first four months. The current interest in health and fitness has brought the Hula Hoop back into popularity.

Did you know?

- The Hula Hoop has been described as the biggest fad of all time.
- At the height of its popularity, Wham-O manufactured 20,000 Hula Hoops a day.
- The Hula Hoop fell from favor in the '60s, but is now popular once more.
- Toy & Game Warehouse offer a pack of 10 assorted Hula Hoops for $110.

IBM Electronic Typewriter

Birthplace: New York, NY

Original Name: Computing-Tabulating-
Recording Company

Incorporation Date: 1911

Hometown Now: White Plains, NY

Original Price: $200 ("Black" model,
12-inch carriage)

IBM Annual Net Income: $8.4 billion

IBM Total Assets: $109.2 billion

Number of IBM Employees: 329,001

IBM founded their Electric Writing Machine Division in 1933 when they took over Electronic Typewriters. They immediately invested over $1 million to redesign the company's Electromatic Typewriter, and launched the IBM Electric Typewriter Model 01 (Improved) in 1935. The one millionth IBM typewriter was delivered in 1958, the twenty-fifth anniversary of the division. The Memory Typewriter was launched in 1974, and 1981 saw the company offer its first PC, which retailed for "as little as" $1,565. The company is now a global leader in the field of IT, which can trace its roots back to the very first writing machine.

Did you know?
- The first patent granted to a typewriting device was issued in 1714.
- William Austin Burt of Detroit, MI, built the first American writing machine.
- The first power-operated typewriter was invented by James Fields in 1914.
- Today's IT product range include notebooks, desktop PCs, and handhelds.

I ♥ NY T-Shirt

Birthplace: New York, NY

Originator: Milton Glaser

Hometown Now: New York, NY

Spokesperson: New York's 51st Governor Hugh Carey

Date Introduced: 1976

Original Price: Unknown

Today's Price: T-shirt $4.99 and up

Number of Products: Countless!

Number Sold: Unknown

The "I ♥ NY" logo was developed to promote tourism to New York in the 1970s, when the city almost went bankrupt. Ironically, although the logo is one of the most successful icons of pop culture ever conceived, designer Milton Glaser waived his fee for its creation. It now appears on a massive range of tourist souvenirs, including the original T-shirt, classic thongs, and T-shirts for dogs. Glaser introduced a updated version of the symbol in the wake of the September 11th tragedy – a wounded heart appeared with the slogan, "I ♥ NY MORE THAN EVER".

Did you know?

- "I ♥ New York" is the official song of New York State, and was written by Steve Karman.
- New York State owns the copyright of the logo.
- The logo is the most frequently imitated design in history.

Jack Daniel's

Birthplace: Lynchburg, TN

Originator: Jasper "Jack" Newton Daniel

Hometown Now: Lynchburg, TN

Date Introduced: 1866

Today's Price: From $25.96

Number of Products: Just whiskey!

Proprietor: Len Motlow

Jack Daniels was born in 1850, one of thirteen children. At the age of seven, he started work for the Call family. Call was a Lutheran minister and whiskey-still owner. Jack learned as much as he could about whiskey distilling, and adopted his mentor's belief in mellowing fresh whiskey through hard maple charcoal, taking the still over at the age of 13.

Jack was a strange-looking man, standing at 5'2", habitually attired in a knee-length frock coat and a broad-brimmed planter's hat. Like many other premium American products, Jack Daniels was introduced to a wider audience at the 1904 St. Louis World's Fair, where it was honored with a gold medal as the world's best whiskey. Jack died from blood poisoningin his foot, in 1911 after trying to kick his safe open. His nephew, Len Motlow, inherited the distillery and continued the family business. The Jack Daniel's distillery is situated in Moore County, Tennessee—dry since prohibition.

Did you know?

- Whiskey loses around 30 percent by volume during the aging process. This is called the Angel's share.
- American white oak is used for Jack Daniel's barrels, giving the drink its smoky flavor and amber tint.

J

Jeep

Birthplace: Butler, PA

Originator: Karl Probst

Hometown now: Toledo, OH

Date Introduced: 1940

Today's Price: $25,275

Original Wartime Production: 700,000
   units

Number of products in present range:

Stock Exchange Symbol: DCX (Daimler
   Chrysler Corporation)

A good design doesn't need much changing, and the similarity between the WWII vehicle and the present-day Jeep Wrangler demonstrates this very clearly. When the U.S. Army was looking for a light vehicle to provide transport, the Infantry Board initially approached

Specifications: Wrangler Sahara

Engine: Six-cylinder Power Tech I-6

Displacement: 242 cubic inches

Power: 190 bhp @ 4600 rpm

Torque: 235 pounds-feet @ 3200 rpm

Transmission: 5-speed manual

Wheels: Ravine Aluminum 15x8 inches

Tires: Wrangler All Terrain

Wheelbase: 93.4 inches (originally
   80 inches)

Overall length: 155.4 inches

Height: 70.8 inches

Width: 66.7 inches

Gross weight: 4450 pounds (1275
   pounds originally)

> *"It's as faithful as a dog, strong as a mule, and as agile as a goat."*
> Ernie Pyle

the Bantam Car Company. The first order of the prototype Jeep, designed by Karl Probst, was delivered in 1940. The Army appropriated Probst's design, and ordered full-scale production at Willys-Overland and Ford, freezing Bantam out of the deal for a staggering 700,000 vehicles. The origin of the name is obscure; but Ford claims that it is from their original designation GP. G for Government and P for an 80-inch wheelbase. Another theory involves Popeye's sidekick Jeep, just like the famous vehicle, he could do almost anything. The first CJ (Civilian Jeep) models appeared after the war, and were made by Willys from 1945–1949. Kaiser then took over the company. In 1970 AMC took over Kaiser-Jeep, and in 1987 Chrysler acquired both Jeep and AMC. But the Jeep tradition has survived, most strongly in the lines of the Wrangler, our featured car.

J Jell-O

First Patented Gelatin Dessert: 1845

Jell-O Named By: Mary David Wait

Birthplace: Le Roy, NY

Rights to Jell-O: acquired by Frank
   Woodward

1906 Sales Value: $1 million

Hometown Now: Northfield, IL

Jell-O Museum Opened: 1997,
   Le Roy, NY

Number of Products: 158 plus

Several attempts were made to launch gelatin **desserts in the nineteenth century, but they all flopped.** School dropout Frank Woodward bought the rights to Jell-O from his neighbor Pearle B. Wait for $450, and started to manufacture the product at his Genesee Pure Food Company. Wait had invented the first fruit-flavored gelatin. Woodward finally managed to get the product off the ground with intensive advertising, and by giving away over 15 million Jell-O cook books. Renamed the Jell-O Company, Woodward merged his assets with those of Postum Cereal in 1925, to form the nucleus of the General Foods Corporation that is now a part of Kraft.

Did you know?

- The Jell-O brand is recognized by 95% of Americans, and is regularly used in 66% of U.S. households.
- Jell-O has no carbohydrates and is used in several "South Beach Diet" desserts.
- Jell-O sponsored the Jack Benny Show for 10 years, while comedian Bill Cosby was a later spokesman for the company.

Jockey Shorts

J

Founder: Samuel T. Cooper

Company Launched: 1876

Jockey Brief Introduced: 1934

Jockey For Her Launched: 1982

Hometown Now: Kenosha, WI

Number of Employees: 5,000

Today's Price: Men's briefs from $7

Number of Products: 16 styles of brief

Company Name: Jockey International Inc.

Remnants of leather loincloths, thought to be over 7,000-years-old, have been unearthed, but it is thought that the men of ancient Egypt may have been the first to wear fabric underwear...under their skirts!

Samuel Cooper's underwear factory began to manufacture men's briefs in 1930, but it wasn't until 1934, with the advent of the Jockey Y-vent brief, that underwear design was revolutionized forever. This was the first time that men were offered an easy-to-use diagonal vent. Although seriously challenged by designer underwear in the '70s and '80s, many men continue to prefer the universally recognized Jockey brief, and can now choose from a great range of styles and price points.

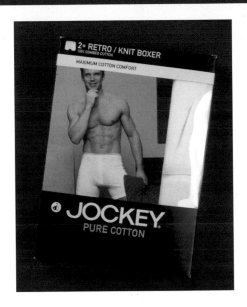

Did you know?

- "Jockey" refers to the "jock strap–like" masculine support that the briefs offer.
- "The Jockey Shorts Effect," which asserts that brief-wearing men are less fertile than their boxer-wearing counterparts, is now thought to be just an urban myth.

John Deere 2-cylinder Tractor

Birthplace: Waterloo, IA

Originator: John Froelich

Company Incorporated: 1868

Hometown now: Moline, IL

Date Introduced: 1935

Today's Tractor Price: $9,000 to
$40,000 plus

Number of Products: 100 plus

Current Sales Value: $19 billion

Stock Exchange Symbol: DE

John Deere was a blacksmith who pioneered the self-cleaning plow and set up his company in 1837 in Grand Detour, Illinois. But the development of the famous tractor was left until 1912, when Joseph Dain was asked to design and build the company's first tractor. But this first attempt was not a success. The tractor was far more expensive to produce than its rivals. The Dain retailed at $1,700 when a Fordson cost less than $700. Another rival, the Waterloo Gasoline Engine Company, had been producing engines and tractors since 1893, when John Froelich and a group of investors founded the company. Their successful 25 hp two-cylinder engine helped to make the Waterloo Boy tractor one of the most popular on the market. Deere & Company bought WGEC for $2,200,000 in 1918, and continued to make the Waterloo Boy tractor until 1923 when the John Deere Model D replaced it. The "D" was still based around the classic twin-cylinder engine, and this engine format survived until 1960. By this time, the market had changed, and demand had grown for larger four- and six-cylinder machines. The featured tractor, the Model B was built from 1935. It was a scaled down version of the Model A, designed as a compact model for small farmers. This market was particularly important to tractor manufacturers, as over a half of all farmers owned less than a 100 acres of land at this time. The John Deere Company is now synonymous with farming machinery and it's famous catchphrase: "Nothing runs like a Deere."

"I will not put my name on a product that does not have in it the best that is in me"

John Deere

Did you know?

- John Deere never lived to see the tractors that bear his name, but the company remains true to his ethic.
- The early tractors were designed to run on kerosene, at only six cents a gallon.
- It wasn't until 1937 that tractors were "styled" by Henry Dreyfuss to reflect the auto styling of the day.

KA-BAR Fighting Knife

Birthplace: Olean, NY

Company Founded: 1897

Originator: Capt. Shuey

Hometown Now: Olean, NY

Date Introduced: 1942

Commentator: Tony Logsdon

Today's Price: $70.73

Number of Products: 103

Number Sold: One million during WWII

Ownership: Private Company

Shortly after the start of World War II, KA-BAR started work in close cooperation with the Marine Quartermaster to produce a fighting knife for the Marine Corps. Careful consideration was given to its design to maximize its effectiveness in battle conditions. The Leather Washer Grip, for example, has recessed rings that allow the user to maintain a grip in wet and slippery conditions. The flat-topped handle end could be used to drive in a stake, and the coated clip point blade, reminiscent of the "Bowie" shape, was useful for both thrusting and hacking.

The knife gained well-deserved respect for its dependability and quality and was adopted not only by the Marines, but also the Army, Navy, and Coast Guard. It was reintroduced in the late 1970s.

Today the original knife remains a favorite with adventurers, survivalists, outdoor sportsmen, and collectors.

"I love my knife, it's never let me down. One day I wrote a song called 'I Wish KA-BAR Made a Truck.' So keep up the good work, and consider making a truck, or maybe a girlfriend."

Tony Logsdon, satisfied KA-BAR customer

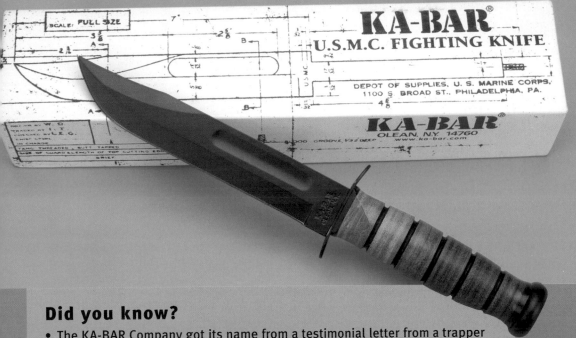

Did you know?

- The KA-BAR Company got its name from a testimonial letter from a trapper who had used one of their knives to kill a bear after his gun had jammed. All that was legible of his scrawled writing was "K. A Bar." The company was so honored by this that it used this phrase as a trademark.
- 1 million knives were produced in the wartime period alone.

K Rations

Birthplace: University of Minnesota

Originator: Ancel Benjamin Keys

Date Introduced: May 1942

Declared Obsolete: 1948

Packaged by: Wrigley Company

Chocolate by: Hershey (2 oz bar)

Other Components: gum, cigarettes, candy, and toilet paper

Number Produced: 105 million in 1944

K rations were developed as basic field provisions for American paratroopers fighting in World War II. The three-meal units were packed into thermoplastic-coated cartons, and were designed to deliver 3,000 calories each day–containing all the nutrition required by a fighting man in small, easy-to-carry packs. Originally, they were designed for emergency consumption for short

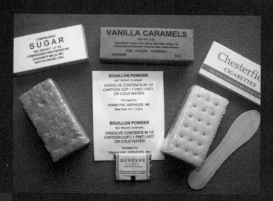

Did you know?

- Ancel Keys and his wife, Margaret, are credited with introducing the Mediterranean diet to the world.
- Keys was known as "Mr. Cholesterol" because of his work on heart disease and nutrition.
- Reproduction K ration kits are now available.

periods of only 2–3 days, in the absence of any other food. This was often abused, however, and many troops lived off the meal kits for many weeks. This led to K rations becoming increasingly unpopular. The calorie intake proved inadequate for men in combat situations. In addition, the fact that their contents lacked "bulk" meant that many combatants felt perpetually hungry. Despite this, some processed foods–such as Spam, Mor, and Prem–jumped out of the ration kits into the stores. The packaged aspect of the rations also had a great influence on the peacetime food industry.

Kazoo

Birthplace: Macon, GA

Originator: Alabama Vest

First Maker: Thaddeus Von Clegg

Kazoo Factory Museum: Eden, NY

Date Introduced: 1852

Date Patented: 1923

Plastic Kazoo: from $1

Metal Kazoo: from $1.99

Wooden Kazoo: from $3.75

Kazoo Museum: San Jose, CA

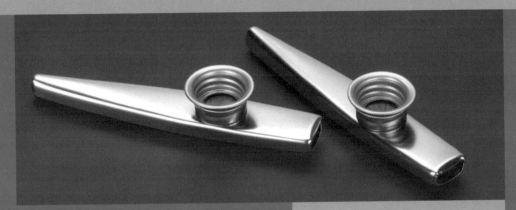

"**Membranophones**" are instruments containing a sliver of material that vibrates when a performer hums or sings into it. The kazoo is an American version of the instrument, whose creator, Alabama Vest, probably witnessed an African slave playing an original instrument in the 1840s. The first kazoos were made in Macon, Georgia, and caught on more widely after 1914, when metal versions (with paper membranes) were introduced by a plant in Eden, New York. Nine years later, Michael McIntyre, a partner in the manufacturing operation, obtained a patent for the design. In 1924, the kazoo made its recording debut when Dick Slevin featured it on the Mound City Blue Blowers' *Arkansaw Blues*. Kazoos went on to be used by jug band, blues, and skiffle artists, but the instrument's simplicity, and the cheapness of the plastic version, has made it most popular as a musical toy.

Did you know?

- Eric Clapton's version of *San Francisco Bay Blues* (on his 1991 *Unplugged* album) features a kazoo solo as tribute to that of the seminal version by Jesse Fuller.

K Kentucky Fried Chicken

Birthplace: Corbin, KY

Originator: Col. Harland Sanders

Hometown Now: Louisville, KY

Recipe Introduced: 1939

First Franchise: 1952, Salt Lake City, UT

Name Abbreviated to KFC: 1991

Reversion To Original Name: 2005

Annual Sales: 1 billion chicken dinners

Chicken Wing (47g): 150 calories

Stock Exchange Symbol: YUM

Harland Sanders had a rough start in life and didn't have any kind of smooth ride to success. His father died when Harland was just six, and he had to take care of his younger brother and sister, while his mother worked in a shirt factory. She taught him how to cook for the family and by the age of seven he had mastered many southern dishes, including fried chicken. After working in a series of low paid jobs, Sanders opened a gas station and started serving fried chicken to his customers. The fame of his chicken grew and he opened his first restaurant, the Sanders Court and Café. He gradually developed his product and began to pressure-cook the chicken to speed up the service. His dishes became so popular that he was made a Kentucky Colonel in 1935 to honor his services to the state's cuisine. But when a new main road bypassed his restaurant, Sanders was ruined. This is when the man showed his true mettle. Living off social security at the age of 65, he invested his modest resources into building up a franchise chain for his chicken recipe. He drove around the U.S.A., keeping his secret spice mixture securely in his car. He managed to build up a franchise network of 200 restaurants, each of which paid him 5 cents for each chicken dinner they sold. Ultimately, he sold out of the business for $2 million. KFC went public in 1966 and is now owned by Yum! Brands Incorporated, the world's largest restaurant company, with over 32,500 outlets.

> *"Fried chicken can, in fact, be part of a healthy diet."*
> 2004 KFC Advertising

Did you know?

- In 2003, *Playboy* model and actress Pamela Anderson urged consumers to boycott KFC in a bid to improve animal welfare.
- Left penniless at the age of 65, Sanders used his $105 Social Security check to launch his franchise business.

Kingsford Barbecue Charcoal

K

Birthplace: Kingsford, MI

Originator: Henry Ford

Hometown Now: Oakland, CA

Date Introduced: 1921

Number of Products: 7

Today's Price: Around $19.99
  (20 lb bag)

Kingsford Leading National Brand

Kingsford Owners: Clorox Company

Clorox is a $3.9 billion business

Barbecues originate from the Western cattle drives of the 1800s, when cowboys slow-cooked the less tender cuts of beef they were given to make them more tasty. Orin F. Stafford pioneered the process of making charcoal briquettes, but it was Henry Ford who transformed this technology into a commercial enterprise. Using wood scraps from his Model T manufacturing plant, he established Ford Charcoal, and had a charcoal plant in full production by 1921. One of Ford's relatives, E.G. Kingsford, managed the briquette operation, and the plant and adjacent workers' village were named in his honor. Kingsford is now the leading charcoal brand in the USA.

Did you know?
- "Barbecue" comes from the Taino Indian word "barbacoa" referring to meat-smoking apparatus.

Kleenex Tissues

Birthplace: Neenah, WI

Originator: Kimberly-Clark

Hometown Now: Neenah, WI

Date Introduced: 1924

Original Price: $0.50

Today's Price: From $2.05

Number of Products: 128 plus

Number of Employees Worldwide:
 62,000

Stock Exchange Symbol: KMB

Four young businessmen, **John A. Kimberly, Havilah Babcock, Charles B. Clark, and Frank C. Shattuck founded Kimberly-Clark in 1872.** They launched the facial tissue in 1924, marketing it as a sanitary way to remove cold cream and make-up. But when the focus turned to selling the tissues as disposable handkerchiefs in 1930, sales soared. Kimberly-Clark introduced the first pop-up tissue carton in 1928, the first colored tissues in 1929, the first pocket packs in 1932, scented tissues in the '80s, "Coldcare" tissues in the '90s, and "Anti-Viral" tissue in 2004. The company's ingenuity means that over 1.3 billion people turn to their products each day. Advertising has also been at the heart of their success. They were one of the first to use radio advertising in the '30s, and their "Little Lulu" character was hugely popular in the '50s and '60s.

Did you know?

- Kimberly-Clark introduced the short-lived paper dress in 1966, priced at $1.25.
- Kleenex present "Tearjerker Movies" on TV, renowned for misty eyes, furtive nose-blowing and downright weepiness.
- Kleenex's Anti-Viral tissues kill 99.9% of cold and 'flu viruses within 15 minutes.

Kodak Brownie

Birthplace: Rochester, NY	Original Price: $1
Originator: Frank A. Brownell	Final Price 1970: $8.95
Hometown Now: Rochester, NY	Number of Products: 125 Brownie models
Date Introduced: 1900	
Spokesperson: Ansel Adams	Stock Exchange Symbol: EK

The Brownie was originally designed to appeal to children, and was named after Palmer Cox's "Brownie" character. Palmer Cox was a famous children's author and illustrator, and his "Brownies" were as famous as Mickey Mouse in their day. He described them as being "like fairies and goblins–imaginary little sprites, who are supposed to delight in harmless pranks and helpful deeds."

The Brownies also had an extensive career in advertising, promoting cigars, coffee, ice cream, and pain-killers. In fact, the Brownie camera revolutionized the whole concept of photography, changing it from a professional to an amateur activity.

Eastman Kodak's low price/high volume manufacturing strategy meant that 150,000 Brownies were sold in their first year of production. The handheld camera led to the birth of the snapshot and began the era of family photography. Over seventy years of Brownie production, many models were introduced, including the Brownie Target, Beau Brownie, Boy Scout Brownie, and Brownie Hawkeye. The final model, the Brownie Fiesta, was made between 1966 and 1970. Every modern technology that uses pictures to communicate, including the internet, can trace its origins back to the Brownie.

"Shortly after our arrival in Yosemite (in June 1916), my parents presented me with my first camera, a Kodak Box Brownie."

Ansel Adams

Did you know?

- Kodak gave away 500,000 Brownies in 1930, one to every child that was 12 in that year, to celebrate their fiftieth anniversary.
- A special Baby Brownie was launched in 1939 to celebrate the New York World's Fair, priced at $1.25.
- Our photo features an early model and a Six-20 Brownie Model F from 1955.

K Kool-Aid

Birthplace: Hastings, NE

Originator: Edwin Perkins

Hometown Now: Northfield, IL

Date Introduced: 1927

Original Name: Fruit Smack

Original Price: $0.10 per packet

Today's Price: Around $0.05 per glass

Number of Products: 11 varieties

Number of Flavors: 33 plus

Stock Exchange Symbol: KFT

Edwin Perkins ran a mail order business and **concocted Kool-Aid by dehydrating his earlier product, Fruit Smack, to make it easy to mail to his customers.** Originally called Kool-Ade, the little packets of unsweetened drink mix became hugely popular, and gradually became the Perkins Products Company's sole merchandise. The original flavors were strawberry, cherry, lemon-lime, grape, orange, and raspberry. Perkins ensured that Kool-Aid survived the Great Depression by halving the packet price to 5 cents. In 1953, Perkins sold the brand to General Foods, who introduced the famous Smiling Pitcher Face in 1954 and sweetened Kool-Aid in 1964. The brand is now owned by food giant Kraft, who are now developing a computer animated Pitcher Man.

Did you know?

- Kool-Aid is the official soft drink of Nebraska.
- "Pitcher Man" was born in 1975.

L.L. Bean

L

Birthplace: Freeport, ME

Originator: Leon Leonwood Bean

Hometown Now: Freeport, ME

Date Introduced: 1912

Annual Sales of $1 million: 1937

llbean.com Launched: 1995

llbean.com Orders: 56,000 per day

Annual Sales 2004: $1.4 billion

Permanent Employees: 3,900

Owner: Family company

Leon Leonwood Bean began his mail order business in 1912, selling the Maine Hunting Shoe from a four-page flier. Surprisingly, this was not an unqualified success, as ninety of the first hundred pairs sold were returned with stitching problems. But Bean snatched success from the jaws of failure by introducing his 100% satisfaction guarantee and repairing the shoes. The boots and guarantee are still available and L.L. Bean is widely recognized for its great customer service. When L.L. died in 1967, still running his business at the age of 94, the company received 50,000 condolence letters.

Did you know?

- L.L. Bean had had its own zip code since 1976.
- Eleanor Roosevelt made a surprise visit to the Freeport store in 1938.
- L.L. Bean removed the locks from the door of the Freeport store in 1951, as it is permanently open.

L Las Vegas Strip

Birthplace: Nevada Desert, NV

Originator: Hotelier Tommy Hull

Hometown Now: Nevada Desert, NV

Date Introduced: 1941

Spokesperson: Norman Mailer

First Strip Hotel: El Rancho Vegas

First Hotel Opened: 1941

Strip Hotels/Casinos: 45

Length of Strip: 3.3 miles

Annual Rainfall: 2 inches

Rafael Riviera was the first known white man to set foot in the Las Vegas Valley and he found it to be a real oasis in the desert, with abundant water. The Valley became a staging point for gold miners, Mormons, and settlers on their way West. Las Vegas itself had rather inauspicious beginnings as a tent town by the side of the San Pedro, Los Angeles & Salt Lake Railroad. But the die was cast when Nevada became the first state to legalize casino-style gambling. This soon became Las Vegas's major source of income, and 43% of the State's income now comes from this activity. The first strip hotel was built on Las Vegas Blvd. in 1941, quickly followed by the Last Frontier,

> *"There was a jewelled city on the horizon, spires rising in the night, but the jewels were diadems of electric and the spires were the neon of signs ten stories high."*
>
> Norman Mailer, *An American Dream*

Did you know?

- The Mirage's Buccaneer Bay features a full-size pirate ship and British frigate.
- The Luxor features a full-size reproduction of King Tut's tomb.
- 100,000 couples are married in Vegas each year. All you need is a $50 license.
- Las Vegas is home to around 600,000 people, but has around 30 million visitors a year.
- Modern entertainers like the Blue Man Group and the Cirque du Soleil are now part of the Las Vegas scene.
- The Las Vegas Neon Museum collects, preserves, studies, and exhibits neon signs from the city.

Thunderbird, and Club Bingo. Frank, Dino, and Sammy were instrumental in bringing entertainment to the town's hotels, and to this day, the hotels themselves are the major attraction in the "megaresort" that is Las Vegas. Of course, gambling also draws people to the City, as does the potential of being married by Elvis in one of Vegas's many wedding chapels.

L Lawn-Boy Yard Tractors

Birthplace: Okauchee Lake, WI

Originator: Ole Evinrude

Hometown Now: Bloomington, MN

Date Introduced: 1934

Zero Radius Price Range: $2,899–$3,999

Walk Behind Price Range: $339–$894

Engines Used: Honda, Tecumseh, DuraForce

Models In Z Range: 5

Models In Walk Behind Range: 13

When Ole Evinrude designed and built his first outboard motor back in 1907, he would have hardly dreamed that he was laying the foundation of a lawn mowing empire. At the time the concept of small gas engines powering gadgets of all kinds was becoming increasingly popular. Evinrude sold his company to Briggs and Stratton in 1926. The company subsequently decided to abandon the outboard motor field, so Evinrude and Stephen F. Briggs decided to combine their resources to establish the Outboard Motor Corporation. They produced the original Lawn-Boy power mower in 1934. An industry breakthrough occurred in 1946, when Joel G. Doyle invented the first rotary blade lawnmower, marketed by his Kansas City, Missouri, Rotary Power Company. Several retailers, including Sears, Roebuck and Spiegel placed large orders for Doyle's revolutionary design. Impressed, OMC bought out Doyle in 1952, and rebranded his mowers as Lawn-Boys. Today, the rotary mower is almost universal. In the post–World War II years, the general rise of affluence (and laziness) meant that ride-on mowers became an essential lifestyle choice! Whatever the size of your yard, a shiny new Lawn-Boy meant that you could hang out with neighborhood dudes like Hank Hill and be one of the boys. Lawn-Boy's most formidable competitor, The Toro Company, bought the brand in 1989.

"Allow the hypnotic hum of the mower's engine to eliminate distraction and help focus on important matters–you."

Mowing Your Way to Zen, the Lawn-Boy Help Leaflet

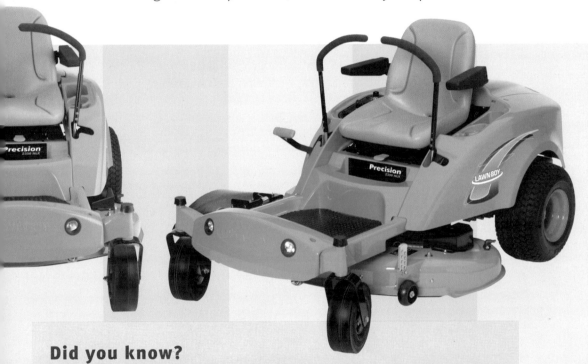

Did you know?

- Ole Evinrude invented his first outboard power unit in 1907, after his future wife's ice cream melted on a long row across a boating lake.
- A high percentage (58%) of Lawn-Boy users remain loyal to the brand when buying new mowers.
- The ZRT is the first riding mower that is specifically engineered to fit each user.

La-Z-Boy Recliner

L

Birthplace: Monroe, MI

Originators: Eward Knabusch and
  Edwin S. Shoemaker

Hometown Now: Monroe, MI

Date Introduced: 1929

Original Company Name: Floral City
  Furniture Company

Coolest Product: Oasis Chair

Latest Marketing Initiative: La-Z-Boy
  Furniture Galleries

When Edward Knabusch and Edwin S. Shoemaker produced their first upholstered recliner in 1929, they named it the La-Z-Boy. The company survived the Depression, and its reputation for craftsmanship grew. In the boom years of the '50s, showbiz stars like Bing Crosby endorsed the recliners, and the company also used sports personalities, figuring that many customers watched TV sport from their armchairs. As lifestyles became more sophisticated, so did the chairs. The featured Oasis Chair (1999), designated "the coolest recliner in America," incorporated a built-in phone, fridge, ten motor massage system, and lumbar heating.

Did you know?

- During the Depression, the company accepted livestock in payment for chairs.
- A La-Z-Boy recliner was the chair of choice for Joey in the TV sitcom *Friends*.
- The company's contribution to the love and peace era of the '60s was a dual reclining loveseat, the Sofette.

Leatherman Tool

Originator: Tim Leatherman	Today's Price: $45
Inspiration: 1975 trip to Europe	Number of Models: 11
Date Patented: 1980	Weight: 1.75 ounces (Micra) to
Hometown Now: Portland, OR	5 ounces (PST II)
Spokesperson: *Stuff* magazine	Warranty period: 25 years

Traveling through Europe in his $500 Fiat car, Tim Leatherman discovered that his scout knife was not the answer to all emergencies; it particularly lacked pliers. On his return to the U.S.A., he spent five years developing the PST—the Pocket Survival Tool. The basic elements that Tim managed to incorporate were both needle-nose and regular pliers, wire cutter, knife, metal and wood files, 8-inch and 20-centimeter rulers, a can/bottle opener, small, medium, and large screwdrivers, and an awl/hole punch. He constructed the tool

from stainless steel so as to avoid corrosion. A further development of the knife, the PST II, saw the addition of a pair of scissors, a serrated knife blade, a diamond coated file, and a sharpener. *Stuff* magazine reviewed the product and concluded that it was "perfect for a guy on the fly." Yes, at the risk of being sexist, this probably is a guy thing.

Did you know?

- A Leatherman Super Tool was used to repair New York Yankee Jorge Posada's mitt in the dugout during the World Series.
- The new Juice C2 was selected for inclusion in the 74th Academy Awards Gift Baskets.

Levi's 501s

Birthplace: San Francisco, CA	Date Patented: May 20, 1873
Originators: Levi Strauss and	Original Price: $0.20
Jacob Davis	Sales Volume (2004): $4.16 billion
Hometown Now: San Francisco, CA	Main Levi Strauss Brands: 3
Date Introduced: 1873	Owners: Privately owned

Levi Strauss (1829–1902) came to New York from his birthplace in Bavaria in 1847. Other members of his family had previously established a dry goods firm in the city, and after working alongside them for about six years, Levi moved to San Francisco, where he set up a prosperous wholesaling business selling fabrics and other merchandise. In 1873, he and one of his clients, a tailor from Nevada named Jacob W. Davis, obtained a joint patent, financed by Strauss, for a method of strengthening "a pair of pantaloons" by "having [their] pocket-openings secured at each end by means of rivets .... whereby the seams .... are prevented from ripping." Almost immediately, Strauss started manufacturing reinforced "waist overalls" (as they were called) to Davis's specifications, eventually assigning them a now-familiar serial number: 501. They proved highly successful as working clothes, but Strauss himself did not live long enough to witness the gradual transformation of his company's robust denim pants, later known as "Levi's", into fashionable leisure wear—a process that probably began when *Vogue* magazine featured them in 1935, and was further boosted by movie stars, pop musicians, and other trend-setters during the '50s and '60s.

Did You know?

- The red tab sewn into the side of the right-hand back pockets of Levi's pants made its debut in 1936.
- In 2001, Levi Strauss & Co. paid $46,532 at auction for a pair of workpants it had made in the 1880s.
- In 2004, the firm proclaimed that May 1 (5/01) would henceforth be officially known as "501 Day."

"*What has happened to denim in the last decade is really a capsule of what happened to America. It has climbed the ladder of taste.*"
American Fabrics, 1969

L Life Savers Candy

Birthplace: Cleveland, OH	Today's Price: $0.79
Originator: Clarence Crane	Number of Products: 48 plus
Hometown Now: Glenview, IL	Stock Exchange Symbol: KFT
Date Introduced: 1912	Calories 16g Roll: 60
Original Price: $0.05	Sugar Per 16g Roll: 13g

Chocolate manufacturer Clarence Crane wanted a candy that would sell in the summer without melting, and had an idea when he saw a pharmacist pressing out pills. By introducing the tiny round hole in the middle, Clarence noticed that the little mint candies reminded him of tiny life preservers, and named them "Cranes Life Savers." He sold the rights to Life Savers in 1913, for the not-so-princely sum of $2,900. The brand's new owner, Edward Noble, marketed the candy brilliantly, and went on to make millions. Many different candies have been added to the Life Savers brand over the years, and "Gummi", "Creme", and "Lollipop" Life Savers are now available.

Did you know?
- The original Life Savers flavor was Pep-O-Mint.
- Life Savers was the first American candy to be wrapped in foil.
- The five-flavor roll was introduced in 1935.
- Sours, Sorbets and Sugar Free Life Savers are now available.

Listerine

Birthplace: St. Louis, MI

Originators: Joseph Lawrence and
   Jordan Wheat Lambert

Hometown Now: New York, NY

Date Introduced: 1879

Original Price: $

Today's Price: $3.59 (8.50 fl oz)

Number of Products: Eleven

Stock Exchange Symbol: PFE

Parent Company: Pfizer

When it was first formulated in 1879, Listerine was used as a surgical disinfectant, named in honor of Sir Joseph Lister who had first performed antiseptic surgery a few years earlier, in 1865. But it was soon discovered that Listerine was particularly effective at killing oral germs. It soon became the first "mouthwash" available over the drugstore counter. Originally, the mouthwash was sold as a breath freshener, but a new claim was made for the product in 1983, that it also fought plaque and thus protected

Did you know?

- Listerine have just introduced a new flavor, Citrus Fresh.
- Listerine is named for the English physician Sir Joseph Lister, the pioneer of antiseptic surgery.
- Listerine is now available in "pocket-paks" to kill oral germs on the move.

teeth. In 1987, Listerine was the first non-prescription mouthwash to earn the Seal of Acceptance from the American Dental Association.

Like many products that have grown up to have iconic status, Listerine has had a history of extremely successful advertising campaigns and slogans, the reflected the concerns of the time. These included "Always a bridesmaid, never a bride" in the '30s, and "The taste you hate twice a day" in the '70s.

Lionel Model Trains

Birthplace: New York City, NY	Current Prices: Layouts from $169.99
Originator: Joshua Lionel Cowen	Slogan: (adopted 1909) "The Standard
Hometown Now: Chesterfield, MI	of the World"
Date Introduced: 1901	Total Number of Trains Sold: 50 million+
Price of First Model Train: $6	Present manufacturer: Lionel LLC

In 1901, New Yorker Joshua Lionel Cowen (1877–1965) created a dry-cell powered model railroad flatcar for a shop window display. It generated immediate public interest, and the same year, the Lionel Manufacturing Company, which Cowen co-owned, began making miniature electric trains for retail sale. Lionel was soon offering a range of locomotives and rolling stock, and in 1906, it introduced a new type of track with a third rail that carried current from a main transformer to its engines.

Lionel's "regular" products were meticulously modeled on real-life prototypes, and relatively expensive — though it survived the Great Depression thanks to a much more modest toy: the wind-up "Mickey and Minnie Mouse" boxcar, launched in 1934 and retailing for just one dollar. After a break in output during World War II, post-war Lionel trains and layouts, boasting smoke generators and other novel features, were big sellers, and by the early 1950s, the firm had become the largest toy manufacturer in the world.

More recently, the brand has enjoyed mixed fortunes. From 1969 until 1986, its trains were made by a division of General Mills; manufacturing rights then changed hands again, before being bought by a group of investors including rock musician Neil Young. In late 2004, Lionel LLC filed for bankruptcy protection, but is now trading normally.

> *"For more than a century, Lionel has been defined by its ability to create the best and most innovative products."*
> Jerry Calabrese, Lionel CEO, 2003

Did you know?

- Lionel's top-selling engine, a model of a GM F3 diesel, debuted in 1948.
- Joshua Lionel Cowen once designed mine detonators for the U.S. Navy.
- Lionel engines were first fitted with steam whistles in 1935.

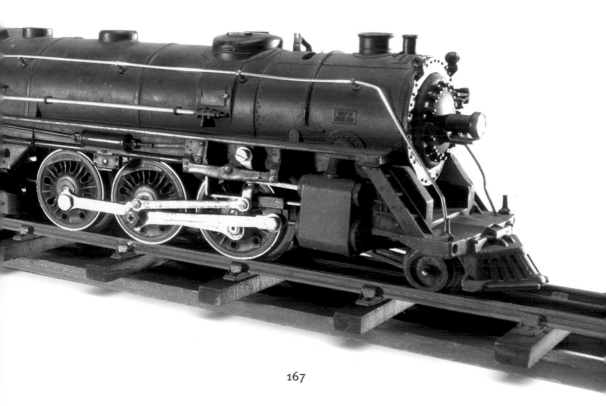

L Louisville Slugger

Birthplace: Louisville, KY

Originator: Bud Hillerich

Hometown now: Louisville, KY

Date Introduced: 1884

Number of Products: 300 base models

Today's Price: Baby's First Louisville
Slugger $5

Number Sold each year: 1.4 million
wooden, and 1 million aluminum bats

Owners: Hillerich & Bradsby Co.

The Louisville Slugger is the most famous bat in the world, and the official bat of Major League Baseball. In fact, it is the "Lumber that Still Powers Our National Pastime" (according to Scott Oldham). The origins of the Hillerich & Bradsby stretch back to the mid-nineteenth century, when German immigrant J. Frederich Hillerich set up a woodturning shop in Louisville, Kentucky. The Hillerich's had left their native Baden-Baden in 1842. Their woodturning shop was soon making every kind of domestic woodwork, from balusters to bedposts, and the shop was employing around twenty workers by 1875. Hillerich's son John Andrew, (who had been born in the US and was known as "Bud") was an amateur baseball player and an apprentice in the family business. Bud used his father's equipment to turn up his own bats, and started making bats for several professional players of the day, including one from white ash for "The Old Gladiator," Pete Browning, in 1884. Browning player for the Eclipse, the Louisville professional team. With this kind of celebrity endorsement, the bat soon grew in popularity and gradually became the signature product of the company. Originally known as the "Falls City Slugger," it

"For more than a century, the Louisville Slugger has been the bat millions of little ballplayers swing the first time they ever step up to the plate"
Scott Oldham

Did you know?

- The Louisville Slugger is used by over 60% of major League Baseball players, including Tino Martinez, Tony Gwynn, and Ken Griffey, Jr.
- Babe Ruth, Hank Aaron, Mickey Mantle, and Roger Maris used the bats.
- The company awards the Silver Bat to the batting champions of the American and National Leagues.

was registered as the "Louisville Slugger" in 1894. In 1897, Bud became a partner in the business, and the company name was changed to J. F. Hillerich and Son. In 1905, the bat became the first sports product to be endorsed by a professional player - Homus "The Flying Dutchman" Wagner of the Pittsburgh Pirates. The Louisville Slugger Museum is one of the most visited attractions in Kentucky, and is easily identified by the six-story, 120-feet long carbon steel bat that casually leans against the building.

M-16 Semiautomatic Rifle

M

Birthplace: Costa Mesa, CA

Originator: Eugene M. Stoner

Hometown Now: Hartford, CT

Commentator: Robert F. Fischer, 9th
  Infantry Division

Date Introduced: 1959

Today's Price: $586

Main Manufacturer: Colt

Primary Function: Infantry weapon

Number Produced: 3,690,000

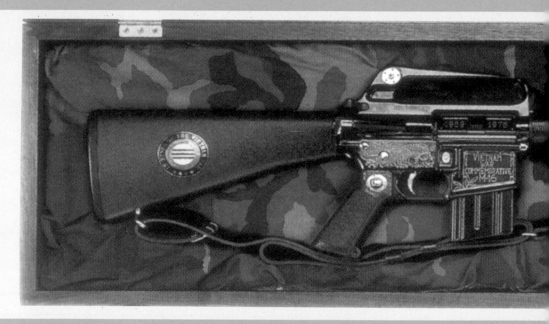

When the M-16 became the standard weapon of the U.S. Army in 1967, it had already undergone some serious testing in combat situations in Vietnam. Personnel like Robert F. Fisher had encountered problems with the open-pronged flash suppressor getting tangled in jungle vines (although they were handy for twisting open the banding on cartons of C-Rats), and with the fouling of the mechanism, which needed regular cleaning.

A series of modifications resolved these problems, and transformed the gun into one of the most reliable and well-liked infantry weapons ever made. The M-16 has also come to be the standard by which all future military rifles will be judged.

*"The early and interim models of the M-16
were oldies but definitely not goodies."*
Robert F. Fischer, 9th Infantry Division, Vietnam

Did you know?

- The gun, which began life as the AR-15 Armalite rifle, was partly inspired by the German World War II Sturmgewehr assault rifle.
- The illustrated rifle is one of a limited edition of 1500, which was manufactured to commemorate the Vietnam War. They are ornamented with gold inlay and plated accessories, and bear the inscription "Lest we forget."

M&M's

Birthplace: Newark, NJ	Number of M&M Colors: 21
Originator: Forrest E. Mars, Sr.	Today's Price: $ 0.75 (1.74oz pack)
Hometown Now: Hackettstown, NJ	Parent Company: Mars, Inc.
Date Introduced: 1941	Number of M&M's Made Each Day:
Date Patented: 1941	400,000,000

While working in Europe during the late 1930s, Forrest E. Mars, Sr. (1904–1999), whose father, Frank C. Mars, cofounded the famous candy company bearing the family name in 1911, had the idea of encasing chocolate drops in a sugary shell to stop them from melting. On his return to the U.S.A., Forrest went into partnership with Bruce Murrie (son of Hershey President William Murrie), and began manufacturing his new confection under the "M&M" brand. Milk chocolate M&M's, made in six colors, debuted in 1941, and quickly became popular with World War II GIs. After the end of hostilities, the candies caught on more widely—from 1950, their maker's identity was reinforced by the "M" stamped on each one. By now, Forrest Mars had taken over Bruce Murrie's 20% stake in M&M, and over the next few years, he promoted his product skillfully, introducing

> *"The milk chocolate melts in your mouth—not in your hand."*
>
> M&M's classic advertising slogan, introduced in 1954

"brand characters" named for the colored candies, bringing in peanut chocolate M&M's in 1954, and making other publicity-conscious moves. Mars's efforts, and those of his successors, have generated widespread affection for the tempting snack: millions of consumers from all over the world voted for a new M&M color in 2002 (purple won), and supplies of the little chocolates have even been taken into space by U.S. astronauts!

Did you know?

- Forrest E. Mars was once so angry about finding a batch of M&M's bearing a slightly less-than-perfect "M" that he demanded their recall.
- Green M&M's are associated with lust and desire.
- During the 1980s, rock band Van Halen introduced a "rider" to their concert contracts, demanding that each venue provide a bowl of M&M's in their dressing room—with all the brown ones removed!

M Mack Trucks

Birthplace: Brooklyn, NY

Originator: John M. Mack

Hometown now: Allentown, PA

Spokesperson: The British "Tommy,"
  World War I

Today's Price: From $100,000

Date Introduced: 1900

Number of Models: 8 in range

2004 Sales: 25,637 units

Stock Exchange Symbol: VOLVY

It all began in 1890, when Jack Mack took a job at Fallesen and Berry Carriage & Wagon in Brooklyn. The era of the horse drawn wagon was fading fast, and after Jack combined with brother Gus to buy out the company in 1893, the brothers began experimenting with electric, steam, and gas motors to drive the trucks they wanted to make. Old No. 1, Mack's first bus, was a 4-horsepower, 20-passenger vehicle that clocked up one million miles in Brooklyn's Prospect Park. That set the standard of reliability which has always been a characteristic of the company. Jack's vision was to produce powerful and durable vehicles that would revolutionize commercial transportation. Their trucks were marketed under the "Manhattan" name until 1910, when the Mack brand was introduced. The first high-volume production model

"The Mack ACs have the tenacity of a bulldog."
British "Tommy," World War I
(The AC Model earned its "Bulldog." reputation for rugged durability in
the trenches of World War I, a heritage that is preserved to this day.)

Specifications: Granite Axle Back Mixer Truck

Engine: Mack, AMI-300 ASET

Power: 325 horsepower @ 1,700–1,900 rpm

Torque: 1,200 ft-lbs @1,300 rpm

Transmission: 8-speed Mack TM308

Front Axle: 12,000 pounds capacity

Rear Axle: 38,000 pounds capacity

Brakes: Dual system air brakes with ABS

Wheels: 22.5x8.25-inch Accuride 10 hole

Tires: 11R22.5x14 inch (duals)

Wheelbase: 192 inches

Weight: 15,903 pounds

was the AB, followed by the legendary AC in 1915. The AC remained in production until 1939. Over 40,000 were built, while being continually improved.

Mack was the first to fit air cleaners and oil filters in 1918, vacuum-assisted brakes in 1920, and rubber mounting blocks between chassis and body in 1922. In 1932, Chief Engineer Alfred Masury made a three-dimensional sculpture of the famous Bulldog logo (which had first appeared in 1922) out of soap during a hospital stay. The resulting mascot still adorns Mack trucks.

M McDonald's

Hometown: San Bernadino, CA	**2005 Fortune 500 Position:** 116
Founders: Dick and Maurice McDonald	**First Quarter 2005 Results:** 6%
Original Restaurant Opened: 1948	increase in revenue
Restaurants Worldwide: 30,000 plus	**2005 Market Value:** $40,453.3 million
Corporate Headquarters: Oak Brook, IL	**Stock Exchange Symbol:** MCD

The McDonald brothers, Dick and Maurice, came to California during the Great Depression, and opened their first restaurant in 1937. Later, they moved to San Bernadino, and set up a drive-in barbecue. At first, the brothers employed a sizeable staff of carhops and cooks; but introduced their newly devised "Speedie Service System" in 1948. They streamlined food production, eliminated the carhops, and offered a menu that was restricted to burgers, fries and milkshakes, all served on disposable paper plates and cups. Profits increased dramatically, and the brothers had to purchase additional catering equipment. Multimixer distributor Ray Kroc was intrigued by their order for a batch of new milkshake machines. He visited the brothers in 1954, and saw their "Speedie Service System" in action. Kroc persuaded the McDonalds to sell him the rights to their brand name and operating methods, and opened his first McDonald's in Des Plaines, Illinois in 1955. Within four years, he owned over 200 McDonald's. By the time of his death in 1984, McDonald's was a global brand with worldwide locations.

"This will go anyplace. Anyplace!"
Ray Kroc, founder of McDonald's Corporation, on first
seeing the McDonald brothers' restaurant in 1954

Did you know?

- Ray Kroc's first day's takings in Des Plaines were $366.12.
- Ronald McDonald first appeared in 1963.
- The Big Mac was the brainchild of franchisee Jim Delligatti.
- The Happy Meal concept was introduced in 1979.
- Ray Kroc led the McDonald's Corporation until his death in 1984, and built the business into a global brand.
- Dick McDonald devised the iconic "Golden Arches."

M | *Mad* Magazine

Originator: Bill Gaines

First Issue: October/November 1952

First Editor: Harvey Kurtzman

Sold To Kinney Corporation: 1960s

Acquired By Time Warner: 1976

Published By: DC Comics

Hometown Now: Manhattan, NY

Original Price: $0.10

Today's Price: Year's subscription $16

Stock Exchange Symbol: TWX

Issues one–three of *Mad* (originally called *Tales Calculated to Drive You Mad*) weren't particularly successful, but the fourth won a wider audience, and the magazine has become America's longest-surviving humor publication. Its original brief was to lampoon American pop culture, but this was soon broadened to include virtually every familiar institution, including the government. From the beginning, the magazine's contributors (or the "Usual Gang of Idiots," as they were affectionately known) included some fantastic writers and illustrators, including Jack Davis, Don Martin, and Wally Wood. *Mad* was plagued by censorship from its infancy, particularly from the Comics Code Authority (established in 1955). This obliged Gaines to convert the comic to a "slick" magazine. Although generally liberal in tone, *Mad* has always been even-handed in its political mauling. In 2001, the magazine accepted advertising for the first time and has used the revenue to boost its color content. Many showbiz personalities say they knew they had made it when they were ridiculed in *Mad*. A famous *Mad* institution is the "Twenty Dumbest People, Events, and Things" of the year.

"*Mad* has affected our culture and history in such an all-encompassing and fundamental way that it is sometime easy to overlook our awesome influence."
Desmond Devlin

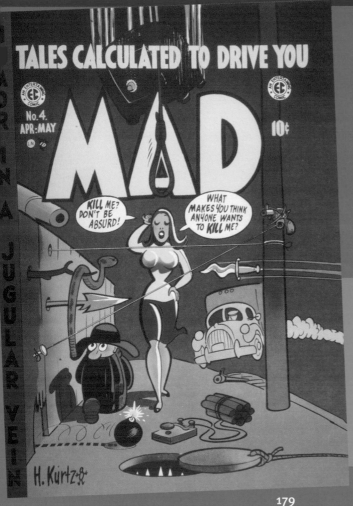

Did you know?

- *The Simpsons* makes frequent references to *Mad* magazine.
- The curly-haired, gap-toothed boy on the cover is Alfred E. Neuman.

M Maglight Flashlites

Birthplace: Los Angeles, CA

Originator: Anthony Maglica

Hometown Now: Ontario, CA

Date Introduced: 1979

Company President: Anthony Maglica

Spokesperson: Judge Ferdinand Fernandez

Today's Price: From $5.91

Number of Products: 6 basic models

"The Mini Maglite was such an elegant piece of engineering and was manufactured to such high quality standards that it took the industry by storm."

Judge Ferdinand Fernandez, judge in Maglite case

A **Croatian American, Anthony Maglica was born in New York and started his company, Mag Instrument, in 1955 with a capital of $125.** Just thirty-five years later, Mag flashlights were nominated as one of *Fortune* magazine's top 100 American products. Starting up as a one-man shop in a Los Angeles garage, Maglica soon spotted a market niche for a reliable, superior flashlight. "The Cadillac of Flashlights" (according to the *Wall Street Journal*) was launched in 1979, aimed primarily at police officers and fire fighters.

Maglica continued to develop and refine the Maglite over the ensuing decades. Maglites were used extensively in Operation Desert Storm, and the company developed special underwater lighting for Jacques Cousteau. The company now sells its products throughout the world, exporting 25% of its output. Mag is so confident in its quality control that its flashlights are offered for sale with a lifetime guarantee.

Did you know?

- Maglites enabled several people to make their way to safety from both towers of the World Trade Center after the aircraft strikes.
- Maglites have appeared in many popular TV series, including *Friends, Baywatch, Clueless,* and *Ellen*.
- Company founder Tony Maglica still supervises the manufacture of all Maglite Flashlights.

M Manco Go Karts

Father of Karting: Art Ingels

Manco Birthplace: Fort Wayne, IN

Company Originator: Bill Hatlem

Hometown Now: Fort Wayne, IN

Date Introduced: 1967

Today's Price: From $649

Number of Products: 11 Karts

Number Sold: One million plus

Current Company Name: Manco Power Sports

The sport of karting was originated in the '50s, reputedly by grounded airmen looking for a fun way to pass the time. Art Ingels is generally accepted as the "father of karting," having built the first true kart in 1956. These original models were gravity powered. But gas, methanol, pressurized gas, and electric karts were all tried out at some time or other. Manco Power Sports is the oldest and largest manufacturer of off-road fun-karts, scooters, mini-bikes, dirt bikes, ATVs, and mini karts in the world. The company has been manufacturing fun vehicles for 38 years, concentrating on safe off-road fun and performance, and has set the industry

Did you know?

- Karting is generally considered to be the most safe and economical motorsport.
- Many NASCAR drivers cut their teeth driving karts, including Lake Speed, Ricky Rudd, Tony Stewart, and Kyle Petty.
- Formula One's Michael Schumacher learned his craft at his father's karting track.

"Manco Go Karts are awesome fun karts for all ages."
Mobileation

standard in these areas. They offer an extensive range of vehicles for every age from six years up, and cater to every level of karting experience, from $649 to $2,995 for the XTK-713E flagship model, which is an adult-sized kart complete with a 404cc engine.

M Marlboro Cigarettes

US Birthplace: New York, NY

Originator: Philip Morris

Hometown Now: Richmond, VA

Date Introduced: 1902

Today's Price: c. $14.95 200-carton

Number of Products: 4 varieties

Inventor of Marlboro Man: Leo Burnett C

Marlboro Box Designer: Frank
 Gianininoto

Stock Exchange Symbol: MO

The Marlboro story is one of the most fascinating marketing stories of the twentieth century, the history of a brand that went from zero to hero with a brilliant campaign that tapped deep into the American psyche. In 1954, the Marlboro brand accounted for less than 1% of the total cigarette market. In fact, it had struggled so badly during the war that it had been taken off the market. Filter cigarettes were thought of as effeminate, and their slogan "Mild as May" had tainted the brand for many men. But a new advertising campaign in 1955, featuring a series of "Marlboro Men," together with a switch to filtered brands from older smokers, caused a huge (5,000%) upsurge in the popularity of the brand. These "Marlboro Men" included a lifeguard, sailor, drill sergeant, construction worker, gambler, and (of course) a cowboy. They were all rugged, lean, healthy outdoorsmen with a masculine dignity, "The Marlboro Man speaks for himself."

The cowboy proved to be the most popular character, and was adopted as Malboro's sole image in 1963. By December 1975, Marlboro was the top selling brand in the US, and is now the most valuable brand in the world with a market worth of $32 billion. Philip Morris cigarette brands now account for 38% of the American cigarette market. Their parent company, the Altria Group Inc., also own Kraft, General Foods, Oscar Meyer and Miller Brewing.

> *"We felt that... we could secure a better understanding and feel of a grass-roots America and what it wanted in a cigarette"*
>
> Joseph Cullman, President & CEO Philip Morris (1950s)

Come to where the flavor is. Come to Marlboro Country.

Did you know?

- English cigarette manufacturer Philip Morris originally established the brand.
- Morris opened his first tobacco shop in Bond Street, London, in 1854.
- The Marlboro brand was named for the London street where the company had its headquarters.
- The "Marlboro Man," Wayne McLaren, died from lung cancer.
- "Marlboro Country" is one of the most widely recognized fictional landscapes in the world.

M Martin Guitars

Birthplace: New York, NY

Originator: Christian Frederick Martin Sr.

Hometown Now: Nazareth, PA

Company Founded: 1833

Moved to Pennsylvania: 1938

Today's Price: $289 - $10,500

Number of Products: 145 plus

Number Sold: 1,000,000 plus

Chairman and CEO: Christian Frederick Martin IV

C.F. Martin & Company is a true family business. It was set up in 1831 by an émigré from Germany, Christian Friedrich Martin. Its current Chairman and CEO, also named C.F. Martin, is the founder's great-great-great-grandson. After his arrival in America, the first Mr. Martin, an experienced guitar maker, ran a

> *"If a famous musician played guitar, he or she played a Martin at some point."*
>
> Tony Tedeschi, *The Christian Science Monitor*, 2003

music shop in New York City for some six years, before relocating to Nazareth, Pennsylvania, where the firm has been based ever since. By the 1870s, some of the Martin characteristic body shapes and decorative features – including the distinctive herringbone-pattern trim that adorns some models– had already appeared. However, it was the introduction of steel strings (replacing classical-style gut) as standard on its instruments in the 1920s that truly established the company's "hallmark" sound. Another important landmark was the launch, in 1931, of its big-bodied "Dreadnought" guitars. Their rich, powerful timbre had proved especially popular with bluegrass, folk and country pickers; and they are still among the most popular of the wide range of models currently in production at Nazareth. Some 170 years after its foundation, the company continues to enjoy critical acclaim and commercial success. In 2004, it announced the completion of its millionth guitar – a "Dreadnought" made from rosewood, spruce, ebony and mahogany, all elaborately inlaid with abalone and precious stones.

Did you know?
- Martin guitar players include Bob Dylan, Joan Baez, Eric Clapton, Paul Simon, Dolly Parton, Martin Carthy and the late Johnny Cash.
- Readers of *Acoustic Guitar* magazine voted Martin the "Most Popular Guitar Manufacturer" of 2004.

M Marvel Comics

Birthplace: New York, NY

Originator: Martin Goodman

Hometown Now: New York, NY

Date Introduced: October 1939

Licensed Characters: 5,000 plus

Original Price: $0.10

Today's Price: From $2.99

Number of Products: Around 13 comics per week

Stock Exchange Symbol: MVL

Marvel Comics grew out of a conglomeration of publishing companies put together by Martin Goodman in the 1930s. The first Marvel comic was published in October 1939, with Joe Simon as editor-in-chief. This first issue featured the Human Torch and Namor the Sub-Mariner. The company also published the patriotic character, Captain America. The company has been through any number of reincarnations in its history so far, finally becoming Marvel Comics in May 1963. The company has had several wobbly financial moments. Sales were decimated in the post-war years, when psychiatrist Dr. Frederic Wertham claimed that comics were harmful to children's development. The company has faced bankruptcy several times, the last in the early months of the new millennium. Despite this, Marvel has created some of the most important comic book characters ever invented, including the X-Men, Superman, Spider-Man, the Hulk, Batman, The Avengers, and the Rawhide Kid.

Over the decades, the company has both set and followed the trends in fantasy writing, and has produced some fantastic artwork. One of the most famous trendsetters was Stan Lee. The company now has a library of over 5,000 proprietary characters, and is one of the world's most prominent character-licensing companies. Although the comic market has dwindled to a fraction of its former size, Marvel remains the largest exponent in the U.S.

> "Like Mickey Mouse and Donald Duck before them, Spider-Man, Superman, and the rest of their cohort became global icons."
>
> David Adesnik, comic expert

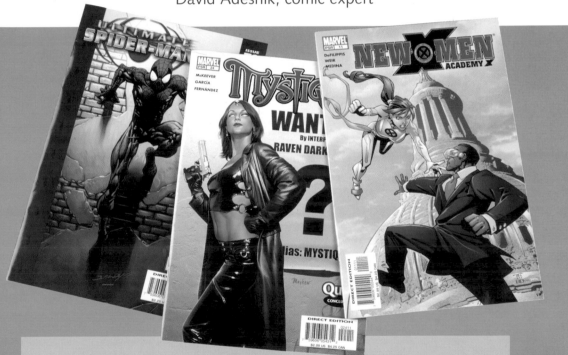

Did you know?

- Marvel has attempted to broaden their reader appeal with *MAX* for mature readers and *Marvel Age* for children.
- Marvel publishes some of their hottest titles on the web as "Dotcomics."
- Comics accounted for only 16.8% of Marvel's net sales for 2004.

Maxwell House

M

Birthplace: Nashville, TN	Total Coffee Market: $18 billion
Originator: Joel Cheek	Brand Owner: Kraft
Hometown Now: Glenville, IL	Kraft Coffee Brands: 10
Date Introduced: 1892	Kraft Parent Company: Altria
Today's Price: $6.99 (39oz can)	Stock Exchange Symbol: KFT

Coffee manufacturer Joel Creek developed a special blend for the Maxwell House Hotel in Nashville, Tennessee, in 1892. It soon became hugely popular, the only coffee served in this prestigious establishment. Postum acquired Joel's company, the Cheek-Neal Coffee Company in 1928, and Maxwell House became one of the founding brands of General Foods/Kraft. The coffee was vacuum-packed as long ago as 1931, the first of many packing innovations for the brand. It has now evolved into many different products, including "Coffee Pods" in 2004. The blend was remastered in 2004, as U.S. consumers now prefer a darker roast.

Did you know?
- President Theodore Roosevelt was served Maxwell House in 1907, and declared it "Good to the Last Drop."
- Almost 80% of Americans drink coffee daily or regularly.
- Maxwell House launched its "1882 Coffee" to commemorate its 100th anniversary.

Mesa/Boogie Amp

Birthplace: Lagunitas, CA

Originator: Randall Smith

Hometown Now: Petaluna, CA

Date Introduced: High-Power 1x12
Combo 1969

Number of Products: 46 plus

Custom Case Options: 84

Mesa/Boogie Artists: Black Eyed Peas,
Bruce Springsteen, David Bowie,
The Rolling Stones, ZZ Top

Randall Smith came from a true **musical background and played in a Bay Area rock band.** He got into amps by mending the one used by his drummer, and found there was a steady market for this kind of work. Randall gradually started to build amps from scratch, and moved into doing this commercially from about 1973. 3,000 Boogies were produced in a mountain shack in his California Hills garden. Mesa/Boogie gradually became a more formal enterprise, dedicated to quality and innovation. The company's

Did you know?

- As Carlos Santana said, "Man, that little thing really Boogies."
- Mesa/Boogie's nickname is the "home of tone."
- 3,000 Boogies were produced in Randall Smith's mountain shack.

products were built in extremely close cooperation with leading players, and were embraced by the guitar playing community. Much more than merely a piece of soulless equipment, the Boogies effectively redefined forever what a guitar could do. There is now a huge roster of Mesa/Boogie artists, from a wide variety of musical backgrounds. The amps are still hand-built by the company in California.

M Mickey Mouse

Birthplace: Hollywood, CA

Originator: Walt Disney

Hometown Now: Burbank, CA

Date Introduced: 1928

First Academy Award: 1932

First Color Movie: 1935 (*The Band Concert*)

Walt Disney Company's Worldwide Box Office Revenues (2003): $3 billion

Stock Exchange Symbol: DIS

Walt Disney (1901–1966) enjoyed **early cartoon success with Oswald** the Lucky Rabbit—and created Mickey (Mortimer) Mouse as a replacement after losing the rights to Oswald in a business dispute. Mickey and his leading lady Minnie made their movie debut in *Steamboat Willie* (1928) and the lovable rodent, whom Disney once described as "a little personality assigned to the purposes of laughter," swiftly became the most widely recognized and popular of all cartoon characters. He has gone on to appear in over 120 movies, and recently featured in a digitally animated Walt Disney video, *Twice Upon a Christmas* (2004).

Did you know?
- The Mickey Mouse Club was founded in 1929, and had more than a million members by 1932.
- Disney himself provided Mickey's onscreen voice from 1928 until 1946.
- Mickey was featured on a 37¢ U.S. postage stamp issued in June 2004.

Microsoft Windows

Birthplace: Bellevue, WA

Originator: Bill Gates

Hometown Now: Redmond, WA

Date Introduced: 1985

Original price: $99 (Windows 1.0)

Today's Price: $199
  (Windows XP Home Edition)

Windows' Estimated Market Share of
  PC Operating System: 95%

Stock Exchange Symbol: MSFT

Windows, Microsoft's Graphical User Interface (see below) for personal computers, debuted in 1985, but did not truly come of age until the arrival of Windows 3.0 in 1990. This version offered adequate levels of file and program management—though, like all GUIs, it demanded considerably more processing power, random access memory and disk space than Microsoft's command line operating system, MS-DOS, with which it still ran in tandem. However, by 1995, an

Did you know?

• Graphical User Interfaces make it possible to control a computer by pointing and clicking at onscreen boxes and icons with a mouse, rather than typing in commands.

• The computer mouse was invented in the 1960s at California's Stanford University by researchers Doug Engelbart and Bill English.

increasing number of machines were capable of taking full advantage of the newly released Windows 95, featuring improved stability, and well-integrated Internet facilities. "95" was also the first stand-alone Windows, with no requirement for a separate MS-DOS. Later editions of the GUI added support for "plug-and-play" and DVD drives, and today, Windows XP is helping to make computing easier and more intuitive than ever.

M Monopoly

Birthplace: Germantown, PA

Originator: Charles Darrow

Manufacturer: Parker Brothers

Hometown Now: Pawtucket, RI

Date Introduced: 1935

Original Price: $4

Today's Price: Deluxe Edition $20.99

Translated Into: 26 languages

Stock Exchange Symbol: HAS

Sold In: 80 countries

Ironically, the most capitalist of all board games was a product of the Great Depression. The stock market crash had reduced inventor Charles Darrow to supporting his family through odd jobs. He remembered the enjoyable summers he had spent in Atlantic City and drew a map of the area on his kitchen tablecloth. He then made play money and constructed little wooden houses and hotels. His friends were soon sitting around his kitchen table nightly, selling real estate and spending stacks of play money. It must have been a refreshing antidote to the financial constraints of their real lives. Parker Brothers bought the game in 1935 and were manufacturing 20,000 copies a week within a month of their agreement.

Did you know?

- Monopoly is the world's most played board game. It is estimated that over 500 million people have played at least one game.
- Parker Brothers brought a lawsuit against Ralph Anspach for his "Anti-Monopoly" game in 1974.
- It is said that Lizzie Magie's 1904 board game "The Landlord's Game" inspired Darrow's invention of Monopoly.

"The game has fifty-two fundamental errors."

Parker Brothers, rejecting Monopoly in 1934

M Moog Synthesizer

Originator: Robert Moog	Hometown Now: Asheville, NC
Manufactured His First Theremin: 1949	Moog Leaves Moog: 1977
R. A. Moog Company Founded: 1954	MiniMoog Voyager Electric Blue:
First Synthesizer Manufactured: 1964	$3,295
Moog Music Inc. Founded: 1971	Moog Documentary: 2004

Robert Moog became interested in electronic music as a student and built his first theremin in 1949. After placing an article in *Electronic World*, Moog received over 1,000 orders, which he filled from his three-room apartment. He then moved on to synthesizers, which generate sounds electronically. He produced his first in 1964, collaborating with musicians Herbert A. Deutsch and Walter Carlos. This was a rare moment in musical

history when a completely new instrument was born. The first synthesizer was monophonic, producing a single note at any one time. Studio technology was used to effect rich and complex sounds. Moog's company continued to develop the synthesizer and created the portable version, the Minimoog. His latest development project is the "interactive piano," complete with touch screen.

Did you know?
- Robert Moog and his musical colleagues starred in the 2004 *Moog* documentary.
- Moog's instruments were the first to combine a piano-style keyboard with artificially generated sound.

Morton Salt

Birthplace: Chicago, IL

Originator: Joy Morton

Hometown Now: Chicago, IL

Original Company: Richmond & Co.

Acquired by Joy Morton: 1886

Morton Salt Company: 1910

Salt Dispenser Patent: 1910

Morton Umbrella Girl: 1911

Today's Price: $0.65 Table Salt (26 oz)

Morton U.S. Plants: 24

Richmond **& Co. began in Chicago in 1845, and become the agents for Onondaga Salt.** As millions of Americans headed west to the California gold rush, buying supplies as they went, the company prospered. Joy Morton acquired the company in 1886, by which time the company was both a salt manufacturer and merchant. Under his innovative leadership, the company developed free-flowing and iodized salts, and introduced the first table salt in 1924. Joy's son, Sterling Morton, coined the advertising slogan "When it Rains, It Pours," and introduced the Morton Umbrella Girl, who still appears on their packaging. Over the years, the company has developed many different specialty salt products for home and industrial use, and is now the leading producer in the U.S. Recent product introductions include lite, seasoned, and garlic salt.

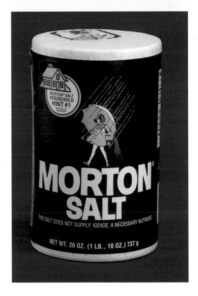

Did you know?

- Judas Iscariot spilled salt at the Last Supper and it has been considered unlucky ever since.
- Lord Howe successfully captured George Washington's salt supply in 1777.
- American salt mining began in the mid-nineteenth century.

M Motorola Portable TV

Birthplace: Chicago, IL

Originators: Paul V. Galvin and
   Joseph E. Galvin

Hometown Now: Schaumburg, IL

Date Introduced: 1950

2004 Value of Sales: $31.3 billion

US Sales: 47% of total

US Patents Granted to Motorola in
   2004: 572

Number of Motorola Employees: 68,00(

The Galvin brothers started the company that was to become Motorola–a Fortune 100 global communications leader – in 1928. The Galvin Manufacturing Corporation first made battery eliminators that enabled radios to be powered by electric mains supply. From the very beginning, the Galvins' ethos was to introduce affordable and desirable consumer goods. They offered the first practical and inexpensive car radio in 1930, naming the product "Motorola" in order to reflect both sound (as per "Victrola") and motion. This was adopted as the company name in 1947, which was also the year that Motorola introduced its first television, the "Golden View VT71", attractively priced at less than $200. This product was hugely successful and sold more than 100,000 units in a year. They offered the first commercially available portable set in 1950 and the 19-inch "Astronaut" (the first large-screen, transistorized, portable television) in 1960. In fact, the period between 1947 and 1954 was the most profitable time in the company's history. Yet, perhaps their most significant contribution to the development of TV was the 1963

Did you know?

• Neil Armstrong's first words from the Moon were relayed 240,000 miles to earth by a Motorola radio transponder.

"Enjoy variety entertainment at home tonight with Motorola Television."
1950 Motorola advertisement

introduction of the rectangular tube. This gave a much sharper picture and remains the industry standard to this day. Sadly, Motorola sold off the Quasar TV division to Panasonic in 1974. The company is now most widely known for its mobile telecommunications products. Interestingly, Motorola has come a full circle, by offering one of the first cell phones with a tiny portable TV on board.

- Motorola was one of the four most successful TV manufacturers in the U.S. by the late '50s (out of 25 companies in this field).
- 98% of U.S. homes have at least one television set, though Motorola no longer manufactures TVs.

M Mr. Coffee Coffee Maker

Birthplace: Cleveland, OH

Originators: Vincent Marotta, Sr.
and Samuel Glazer

Hometown Now: Rye, NY

Date Introduced: 1972

Number of Products: 65 coffee makers

Coffeemaker Sizes: 1 cup – 45 cup

Annual Revenue: $2.6 billion

Employees: 9,000

Stock Exchange Symbol: JAH

The history of coffee drinking is linked with innovative ideas, including the Melita coffee filter (1912) and the Gaggia espresso machine (1946). But Mr. Coffee was the first to market the automatic drip process in 1972. Almost immediately, it became the most successful coffee machine in the U.S.A., selling over 38,000 units a day by 1975. Mr. Coffee has retained this pre-eminent position to this day, and has used its market position to introduce related products. These include the Iced Tea Pot (a completely new product category) in 1989, a water filter in 1992, a hot chocolate maker—and Mrs. Tea, a hot tea maker, in 1995. Jarden Consumer Solutions bought Mr. Coffee's parent company, American Household, in 2004.

Did you know?

- Joe DiMaggio became a spokesperson for Mr. Coffee in 1974.
- Mr. Coffee launched a coffee saver feature in 1977 when the price of coffee tripled.
- The first ever coffee maker was the Turkish "ibrik," circa AD 575, designed to be heated in the desert sand.

Mr. Potato Head

M

Birthplace: New York, NY

Originator: George Lerner

Hometown Now: Pawtucket, RI

Date Introduced: 1952

Number of Products: 11

1953: Mr. And Mrs. Potato Head were married

1974: Mr. Potato Head doubled in size

Today's Price: Darth Tater $7.99

Brand Owner: Hasbro Inc.

George Lerner invented the original Mr. Potato Head. It was an all-plastic toy used as a cereal premium. Hasbro bought the rights to the toy and brought out their own version with a Styrofoam body. A plastic body was added in 1960. Mr. Potato Head played a starring role in Disney's *Toy Story* (1995) and *Toy Story 2* (2000), and launched Burger King's "Try the Fry" campaign in 1997. The toy celebrated its fiftieth anniversary in 2002 by launching special, limited-edition versions, including "Patriotic Mr. Potato Head." "Darth Tater" was launched in 2005, to celebrate the Star Wars movie *The Revenge of the Sith*. "Spud Trooper" is planned for Fall 2005

Did you know?

- Mr. Potato Head lost his pipe in 1987, to become the official "spokespud" of the American Cancer Society.
- Mr. Potato Head received four votes in the 1985 mayoral election in Boise, Idaho.
- Mr. Potato Head was the first toy to be advertised on television.

Nathan's Famous Hot Dog

N

Birthplace: Coney Island, NY

Originator: Nathan Handwerker

Hometown Now: Westbury, NY

Date Introduced: 1916

Spokesperson: Cary Grant

Original Price: $0.05

Nathan's Coney Island Deli Mustard:
$2.05 (16 oz)

Official Hot Dog: New
York Yankees

When Polish immigrant Nathan Handwerker started his hot dog business in 1916, he was probably unaware that his product would become a New York tradition that would spread nationwide. His first nickel stand, on the corner of Surf and Stillwell Avenues in Coney Island, NY, sold his famous 100% beef frankfurters, seasoned with a blend of spices and garlic. Al Capone was a regular visitor, and as the chain grew, Cary Grant was employed to advertise Nathan's by wearing a sandwich board! Nathan's Famous Hot Dogs—and their equally famous Krinkle Cut French Fries—are still the most popular and recognizable menu items in the outlets. Nathan's also sells hot dogs and deli-style fixings for home consumption. The famous "franks" have an incredibly devoted following, and one customer has even named their dachshund "Nathan" for the brand.

Did you know?

- Nathan's annual hot dog eating contest began back in 1916.
- New York City Mayor Rudy Guliani declared Nathan's as "the world's best hot dogs" in 1999.

Nerf Ball

Inventor: Reyn Guyer	Date Introduced: 1969
Manufacturer: Parker Brothers	Today's Price: Turbo Jr. Football $3.99
Founder: George S. Parker	Number of Nerf Products: 31
Company Birthplace: Salem, MS	Number Sold: 4 million balls in the
Hometown Now: Pawtucket, RI	first year

Parker Brothers is an extraordinary games company, with such classics as **"Monopoly" (1935),** "Sorry" (1934), and "Trivial Pursuit" to their credit. Probably their most famous toy (rather than board game) is the Nerf ball–"the world's first official indoor ball." The original Nerf ball, launched in 1969, was just 4 inches across, and made from polyurethane foam. The larger

"Super Nerf ball," "Nerfoop," and "Nerf Football" soon followed. This classic foam technology has now also been applied to the N-strike range of harmless, Nerf-loaded toy guns, "The Ultimate in Ball-Blastin' action" for children and adults, "loads of fun–classic Nerf stuff."

Did you know?
- Reyn Guyer also invented the classic game Twister.
- Parker Brothers invented their first game in 1883.
- Since then, they have invented over 1,800 games and puzzles.
- Nerf crossbows, javelins, and dart guns are also available.

New York Yankees

N

Birthplace: Hilltop Park, Manhattan

Originators: Frank Farrell and
   Bill Devery

Cost of Original Purchase: $18,000

First Game: April 18 1923

Hometown Now: Yankee Stadium, 161st
   Street and River Avenue, The Bronx

Capacity: 57,545

Number of World Series Wins: 26

Ownership: George Steinbrenner et al.

What Yankee fan wouldn't give their right arm to take a trip back in time to that spring afternoon of April 30, 1903, when the Highlanders, as they were then known, played their inaugural home game at Hilltop Park, Manhattan? What hints of the greatness to come would be apparent in the game they won 6-2 versus Washington? Named Hilltop for its elevated position, the traditional, all-wood stadium at 168th Street and Broadway was the first of many famous parks that the team would use in its 100-year-plus history. Even as we pen this article, another ballpark has been announced right across the street from the present Yankee Stadium.

In 1912, the team uniform gained its distinctive pinstripes; and in 1913, when the team moved to the Polo Grounds, also the home of the New York Giants, they officially became the Yankees. In 1920, they purchased a player who would draw record crowds to their games. The team paid $125,000 to the Boston Red Sox to buy out the contract of one George Herman "Babe" Ruth. A new stadium was planned in 1921 and completed April 18, 1923. On opening day, a record crowd of 74,200 watched the Yankees beat the Red Sox 4-1, with the help of a home run from Ruth. Other great Yankee players followed, including Lou Gehrig, Joe DiMaggio, Mickey Mantle, and Reggie Jackson.

Today, the Yankees enjoy cult status and an industry that has grown up around them to provide all manner of branded products.

> *"Babe Ruth, the Superman of Swat –*
> *most picturesque of ballplayers, the greatest*
> *slugger who ever lived."*
> *Baseball Magazine*, September 1927

Did you Know?

- The original Yankee Stadium was built on 10 acres of land purchased from the Astor Estate for $675,000.
- On May 17, 2002, Jason Giambi joined Babe Ruth as the only other Yankee to hit a walk-off grand slam with the team down by three runs.
- Lou Gehrig played in 2,130 consecutive games, a record that stood until 1995 when it was broken by Baltimore's Cal Ripken, Jr.

Nike Air Jordan

N

Originator: Marion Frank Rudy

Hometown Now: Nike Headquarters,
   Beaverton, OR

U.S. Patent: 4219945

Date Introduced: 1985

Commentator: Charlie "The
   Sneaker Freak" (website)

Number Sold: 20 versions of
   original "Air"

Original Price: $65

Nike started in 1962 as a partnership between University of Oregon Coach Bill Bowerman and University of Oregon student Phil Knight. The pair began their business venture by importing high-tech athletic shoes from Japan. But they soon began to adapt these shoes and develop their own lines. The iconic Air Jordan basketball shoes were first offered in 1985, and were re-issued in 1994, 2001, and 2003. Michael "Air" Jordan directly inspired the design, but designer Marion Frank Rudy developed the air-cushioning technology behind the brand. The system relies on pressurized gas encapsulated in the polyurethane, which is designed to gradually inflate over time. This technology was registered under several U.S. patents, the first being 4219945, and has resulted in some of the best athletic shoes ever developed. Nike has produced many spin-off lines, including Air Jordan trainers, and Woman's Jordans (no "Air") in 1998.

> *Sneakerjacking: the "Taking of ones athletic shoes by force or violence. Usually the sneakers in question are Nike Air Jordan models."*
> Charlie, "The Sneaker Freak"

Did you know?

- Nike is the Greek goddess of victory.
- Former President Bill Clinton has at least one pair.
- "Nike knee" is a condition suffered by runners wearing excessively cushioned shoes.
- The "Jumpman" logo is based on Michael Jordan's jumping profile.
- The latest version of the "Air" shoe, the Air Jordan 20, retails for around $175.

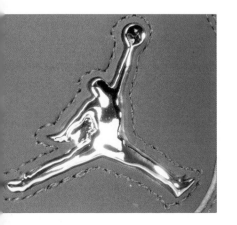

Ironically, "His Airness" Michael Jordan (who most notably played for the Chicago Bulls and the Washington Wizards), started his career wearing Converse basketball shoes—the brand has been owned by Nike since 2003. The development of the Air Jordan range has been one of the pillars of Nike's huge success, and will almost certainly continue to be a significant product for the company. Nike is now the largest sports and fitness company in the world, and has achieved the unusual status of being completely recognizable from an abstract logo.

Nylons

N

Originator: DuPont

Inventor: Wallace Hume Carothers

Nylon Patented: 1937 by DuPont

Nylon Introduced: 1939 New York
World Trade Fair

Nylon Stockings Introduced: May 15, 1940

First Day Stockings Sales: 780,000 pairs

First Year Stockings Sales: 64 million pairs

Invention of Lycra: 1959

Stock Exchange Symbol: DD

Once it became acceptable for women to show their legs in public, the demand for better-fitting legware stimulated the development of the first synthetic fibers. DuPont patented the name "nylon" in 1937 and the first nylon stockings were launched to massive acclaim in 1940, becoming an instant commercial success. At this time, nylon had no stretch, so that stockings were "fully fashioned" to fit the shape of the leg. When WWII interrupted the civilian supply of the fiber, "nylons" became a highly prized commodity. When Dupont went on to invent the stretchy fiber it called Lycra in 1959, the fit of stockings was hugely improved. Glen Raven Mills of North Carolina introduced pantyhose in 1959. These became hugely popular,

Did you know?

- Originally called "Polymer 6.6," nylon got its new name (including the state's initials) at the New York World Trade Fair in 1939.
- Nylon was the world's first synthetic fiber and its commercial production began in 1939 at DuPont's Seaford, plant in Delaware.
- During WWII, nylon was diverted to produce tents and parachutes for the military.
- The on-screen tornado in *The Wizard of Oz* (1939) was made from nylon fiber.

"Women want men, career, money, children, friends, luxury, comfort, independence, freedom, respect, love and cheap stockings that don't run."

Phyllis Diller

especially following the U.K. designer Mary Quant's introduction of the miniskirt in the '60s. Indeed, pantyhose soon accounted for over 70% of

the hosiery market, and many women saw them as a symbol of liberation. Both stockings and pantyhose were now knitted in tubes rather than in flat configuration. This led to the seam becoming defunct by 1965. Yet, stockings retain a special glamour and allure that pantyhose don't have—and recent years have seen a surge in their popularity. As Candice Bergen says, "A real lady always wears stockings. It doesn't matter how hot the weather is."

Oakley Sunglasses

O

Originator: Jim Jannard

Hometown Now: Foothill Ranch, CA

Most Famous Employee: Lance Armstrong

Date Introduced: 1975

Spokesperson: *Forbes* magazine

Today's Price: Men's sunglasses $120 to $435

Number of Products: Over thirty

Oakley Retail Stores: 36

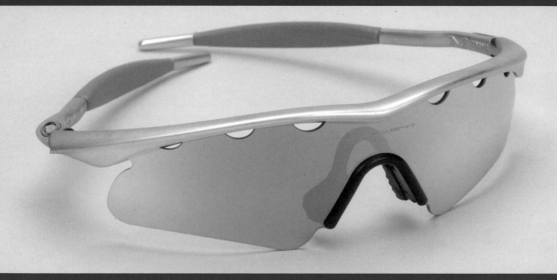

Oakley is a relatively new U.S. brand, having started out in 1975, but it has quickly become one of the thirty premium brands in the world (according to *Forbes* magazine). Their first exposure to their typical customers came through their revolutionary sunglass design, which continues to this day. The company launched their "Thump" musical eyewear in 2005 (as worn by Lance Armstrong), in seven color combinations. The company's products very much reflect the California lifestyle of beach life, surfing, mountain biking, and the great outdoors.

Did you know?

- Oakley offers a solid gold watch for $25,000.
- Oakley sponsors "Big Days Out" in the great American outdoors.

Oreo

O

Hometown: New York City, NY

Originator: Nabisco

Hometown Now: (Kraft Headquarters)
   Glenview, IL

Date Introduced: 1912

Number of Products: Several Oreo
   derivatives, including "Double Stuf,"
   Kosher, and seasonal Oreos

Total Sales: 362,000,000 plus

Stock Exchange Symbol: KFT

The Oreo was one of three new varieties of biscuit launched by Nabisco in 1912. Two of these, the "Mother Goose" and "'Veronese," survived for barely a decade, but the distinctively embossed Oreo, with its seductively sweet center and intriguingly mysterious name, has gone on to become America's favorite cookie— thanks, in part, to classic ads like the "twist, lick, and dunk" campaign that showed us all how we should eat one!

Did you know?

• The meaning of *Oreo* remains a mystery. Is it *or* (French for *gold*) a reference to the original gold-colored packaging, or does the *re* stand for the crème between the two outer *os*?

Orvis

Birthplace: Manchester, VT	Complete Fly Selection: $250
Originator: Charles F. Orvis	Sales in 1965: $50,000
Hometown Now: Roanoke, VA	400th Dealer: 1988
Company Established: 1856	Sales in 1993: $100 million
Today's Rod Prices: $89–$1,095	President & CEO: Perk Perkins

The Orvis family has been in the U.S.A. for a very long time and records take their arrival to before 1640. Charles Orvis was born in the Green Mountains of Vermont, the fourth of seven children. Growing up in this rural location, Charles had a strong interest in field sports from an early age, and he soon started to build his own fishing rods. Both he and his brother were originally hoteliers in their native Manchester,

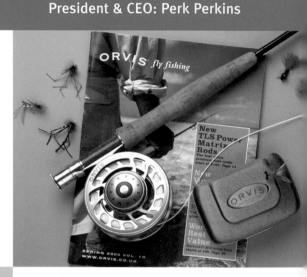

Did you know?

- *Men's Journal* voted Orvis's Vortex rod the "Reel of the Century" in 1999–2000.
- Orvis's daughter, Mary Orvis Marbury, wrote *Favorite Flies and Their Histories* in 1892, and exhibited her flies at the Chicago World's Fair in 1893.

Vermont, but when he became financially comfortable, Charles decided to turn his rod-building hobby into a business. Affluent sportsmen bought the rods while they were on holiday in the area, and continued to buy Orvis goods via mail when they returned home. As well as making the prototype for the modern flyreel, Orvis has been responsible for many other innovations, including the first waterproof bamboo rod (1946), the "Zinger" (1967), the CFO superlight flyreel (1972), and graphite rods (1974).

Otis Elevators

O

Birthplace: New York, NY	Annual Sales: 100,000 elevators
Originator: Elisha Graves Otis	and escalators
Safety Elevator Invented: 1857	2004 Revenues: $9 billion
Otis Brothers & Co. Founded: 1867	Share of World Market: 28%
Elevator Installations by 1873: 2,000	Number Sold: 1.7 million

Steam and hydraulic elevators were already in use by the 1850s, but Elisha Graves Otis invented the first ever safety elevator in 1857. His first elevator was installed in New York, and the idea was immediately popular. By 1873, some 2,000 office buildings, hotels, and department stores across America were equipped with Otis elevators. Their invention facilitated the introduction of high-rise buildings that were to change the American skyline forever. Otis introduced their gearless traction engine elevator in 1903, and this made even taller skyscrapers possible, like the Empire State Building. Otis's products were so robust that they outlasted many of the buildings in which they were installed. Elevators are now common-place, moving the equivalent of the world's population every 72 hours. Nevertheless, Otis continues to make a fundamental contribution to the shape of American cities.

Did you know?

- Otis elevators are fitted in 11 of the world's 20 tallest buildings.
- Otis elevators are fitted in the Chrysler Building, the Luxor Hotel, and the John Hancock Center.

Pendleton Shirt

Birthplace: Salem, OR	Woolen Plaid Shirts: From 1924
Originator: Thomas Kay	Number of Products: 8 woolen
Hometown Now: Portland, OR	shirt styles
Pendleton Founded: 1863	Owner: Family company
Indian Blankets: From 1895	Pendleton-Owned Retail Outlets: 53

Thomas Kay, an immigrant weaver from England, founded Pendleton in 1863, but the company really took off when his daughter, Fannie, married merchandising expert C. P. Bishop. To this day, the company manages a complete vertical manufacturing process, from fleece to retail. The company also remains close to its frontier heritage, offering a wonderful range of saddle and traditional "Indian" blankets. Pendleton originally traded these for silver and other valuables with the Native American tribes of the Northwest. The woolen plaid shirt has been a Pendleton signature classic from 1924 and is now available for women.

Did you know?

- The Beach Boys were originally called the "Pendletones" in honor of the iconic plaid shirt.
- Pendleton was founded in 1863, the year of the Gettysburg Address.
- The fifth generation of the Bishop family runs Pendleton.

Pez Candy Dispenser

P

Birthplace: Vienna, Austria

Originator: Edward Haas III

Date Introduced: 1927

Moved To U.S.A.: 1952

Hometown Now: Orange, CN

Annual U.S. PEZ Consumption:
  3 billion candies

PEZ Dispenser Price: From $1.95

Giant PEZ Dispensers: $19.95

New Flavors: SourZ and Cola

It's strange to think that something as fun as PEZ was originally conceived as a breath-freshening aid for smokers. The candies were introduced as striped mints and sold in a small tin. But a new dispenser designed to look like a cigarette lighter was introduced in 1947, and the product became more recognizable. PEZ moved to the U.S.A. in 1952, and immediately realized that children are the biggest candy consumers. Haas introduced a range of fruit flavors to appeal to his younger customers, and added character heads to his dispensers, including Popeye, Mickey Mouse, Santa, and Dino, the Flintstones' dinosaur. Feet were added in 1987. There is now a thriving collectors' market (of so-called "PEZheads") for this American pop-art classic. A record $6,575 was paid for a PEZ dispenser in 2002.

Did you know?

- PEZ comes from "pfefferminz," German for peppermint.
- PEZ celebrated its fiftieth anniversary in 2002 with the Golden Glow PEZ dispenser.

P Pinball

Birthplace: Chicago, IL

Originator: Raymond J. Maloney

Hometown Now: Chicago, IL

Date Introduced: 1931

Date Name Coined: 1936

Based on: Bagatelle, Victorian parlor game

Original Companies: D. Gottleib, Bally Corp, Bingo Novelty Co.

Surviving Manufacturer: Stern Pinball

The original pinball machines were tabletop models. As they took up valuable bar space, they were initially less popular than slot machines, which could be wall mounted. They also cost twice as much to manufacture, so the profit-space ratio was lower. The definition of what is entertainment and what is gambling has always been a gray area. It is rumored that crime syndicates rigged early pinball machines to pay out money, and the game was unfairly judged one of chance rather than skill. As late as 1942, New York City Mayor Fiorello Henry La Guardia smashed up pinball machines in front of an enthusiastic crowd, to herald the start of a thirty-four year pinball ban. In fact, true aficionados spend hours mastering the technique, honing reaction skills that would send the score digits flying.

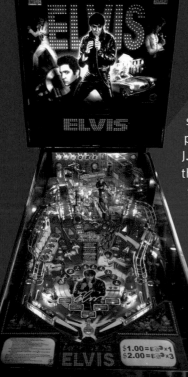

In the famous portrayal of the "Pinball Wizard" in the Who's rock opera, *Tommy*, the Wizard displays a skill of supernatural proportions. The machine he plays is a Bally, produced by the pinball industry founder. In 1931, Raymond J. Maloney of the Lion Manufacturing Corporation developed the Ballyhoo model. Lion became the Bally Corporation in 1968, and income from video arcades and electronic games accounted for over half the company's revenue by the late '70s. Showing the same talent for groundbreaking new ideas that they displayed back in 1931, the company once again led the market with games like "Space Invaders" (1979) and "Pac Man" (1980). Pinball machines have finally become an accepted part of American pop culture.

*"Always gets a replay, never tilts at all,
that deaf, dumb, and blind kid
sure plays a mean pinball."*
Pete Townsend, Pinball Wizard

Timeline

1931 "Ballyhoo" machine released by Lion

1933 First machine to use electricity

1934 "Tilt" warning added

1937 "Bumper" invented

1947 First "flipper" installed

1948 "Flipper" placed at the base of the playfield

1950 Gottleib introduce inward facing "flippers"

1960 Players able to gain extra ball

1962 First "drop targets" on William's "Vagabond"

1979 First talking game, "Gorgar" by Williams

1991 First game to feature dot-matrix display, Data East's "Checkpoint"

Piper Cub

P

Birthplace: Lock Haven, PA

Originator: William Thomas Piper

  "The Henry Ford of Aviation"

Hometown now: Vero Beach, FL

Date Introduced: 1937

Number Made: J-3 14,000 plus

Number Made: L-4 5,677

Descendant: PA-18 Super Cub

1937 Piper Production: 687

1938 J-3 Price: $1,300

"**Piper Cub" is synonymous with "light plane" in exactly the same way that "Hoover" is with the "vacuum cleaner".** This pint-sized classic was designed for flight training, and many WWII fighter aces cut their teeth at its controls. The J-3 first flew in 1937 and was popular for both training and leisure flying. But the onset of war thrust the plane into a completely new role. The U.S. Army renamed the plane the L-4, and the military used it for observation and liaison. 5,677 L-4 Cubs were purchased, along with similar planes from Aeronca and Taylorcraft. Their purpose was to enable commanders to keep in direct contact with their forces, provide vital aerial reconnaissance, and to direct artillery fire. Ironically, the handy L-4 also flew with the Luftwaffe, who captured and operated several examples after the fall of Denmark. Its originator, William Thomas Piper, had entered the aviation industry in 1929, by investing in Taylor Brothers Aircraft Corporation. The resulting airplane was the Taylor Model E-2 Cub, a direct forebear of the Piper J-3. By 1937, Piper had bought out the Taylor Brothers and had begun his quest to bring light planes to the masses.

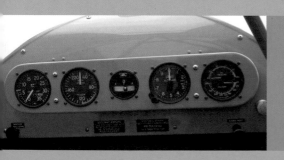

Specifications: L-4, 1945

- Wingspan: 35.21 feet
- Length: 22.38 feet / Height: 6.67 feet
- Gross Weight: 1,220 pounds
- Engine: Continental C90

"When you've flown a Cub, you may find that you are spoiled for anything less."

Dan Ford, *Piper Cub Forum*

- Power: 90 brake horsepower
- Top speed: 87 mph
- Cruising Speed: 73 mph
- Ceiling: 11,500 feet
- Range: 220 miles

P Playboy

Originator: Hugh Marston Hefner

First Issue: December 1953

Investment Capital: $600

Original Price: $0.50

First *Playboy* Club Opened: 1960

2002 Revenues: $278 million

Playboy CEO: Christie Hefner

Playboy Editor-in-Chief: Hugh Hefner

Playboy Circulation: 3 million

Stock Exchange Symbol: PLA

Hugh Hefner came from a strict **Methodist background, but become a founding member of the sexual revolution.** He published his first magazine in November 1953, a potent mixture of humor, good writing, and sex. The first issue sold 53,991 copies. Art Paul, *Playboy*'s first art director, designed the rabbit head motif, and this has appeared on every magazine since the second issue. The publication became the cornerstone of an extensive entertainment empire, which continues to develop. The latest Playboy enterprise is a $50 million casino, which is being constructed in Atlantic City, New Jersey.

Did you know?

- *Playboy's* first centerfold was Marilyn Monroe.
- The best-selling issue ever was November 1972, with a circulation of 7,161,561 copies.
- Hef's private DC-9 jet was called the "Big Bunny."

Polaroid

Polaroid Corporation Founded: 1937

Originator: Edwin Land

Hometown Now: Waltham, MA

Date Introduced: 1948

Polaroid Swinger Launched: 1965

Polaroid One Step Launched: 1977

Number of Products: 19 cameras

NYSE Trading Suspended: 2001

Current Owners: Petters Group
Worldwide

Edwin Land was an inventor and physicist who created a unique process for developing and printing photographs dubbed Polaroid. He collaborated with designer Henry Dreyfuss to produce the Automatic 100 Land Camera and the Polaroid Swinger. The Polaroid X-70 camera of 1972 was a further leap forward. It was the first instant camera to have integral film. The Polaroid One-Step model of 1977 was the world's best-selling camera of the time. In the early '80s, Polaroid brought a dramatic, five-year legal action against Kodak for copyright infringement. Kodak lost in 1985, and was forced to retire from the instant picture market. But then digital cameras completely changed the market and Polaroid went bankrupt in 2001. It continued to trade, however, and is now owned by Petters.

Did you know?

- The intense, slightly surreal Polaroid colors appeal to many artists.
- William Wegman uses a large-format Polaroid to photograph his dogs, Man Ray and Fay Ray, wearing dresses.
- Andy Warhol used his Polaroid to photograph thousands of genitals.

Pontiac GTO Judge

Birthplace: Detroit, MI	Today's Price: $30,800
Originator: Pete Estes/John DeLorean	Engine Specification: Ram Air V-8
Hometown Now: Detroit, MI	Horsepower: 370
Date Introduced: December 1968	Options: Hardtop and convertible
Original Price: $3,161	Number Sold: 6,725

Pontiac's slogan for the 1969 GTO Judge was "Born Great," but the inspiration for the model name actually came from the "Here Come de Judge" skit on *Rowan & Martin's Laugh-In*. It was designed to give young drivers a lot of automobile for the money: it was a fully loaded true muscle car that you could either drive or drag-race. The Judge was a new $332 option package for the '69 GTO.
It came complete with 366 horsepower, Ram Air III induction, and a 400-cid V-8 linked to a three-speed gearbox controlled by a Hurst T-handle shifter and 3.55:1 rear axle. For $390, the buyer could step up to 370 horsepower with Ram Air IV. With this option, the car could cover a quarter mile in 14.45 at 97.80 mph.

The GTO Judge was decorated with loud decals, and was a "hairy" looking car indeed. The first 2,000 examples were finished in a true pop-art color, Carousel Red, and came complete with an extrovert 60-inch-wide spoiler, black-out grille, and stripes—an in-your-face decorative style that became a muscle car tradition. The Judge was designed to mop up customers who were looking for something with more glamor and power than the regular GTOs, and was an attempt to halt the decline in the model's fortunes...though it was only temporarily successful in doing so. The car was highly regarded in its own right, but its hot image did not seem to reflect well on the rest of the range, and GTO sales slid by nearly 20 per cent for the '69 model year. Worse

was to come. A combination of the energy crisis and spiraling insurance costs—generated by muscle cars' scary performance image—meant that young drivers just couldn't afford the very model designed to appeal to them. The demise of the Judge heralded the end of the muscle car era itself.

"The GTO combined brute, blasting performance with balance and stability of a superior nature."

David E. Davis, *Car and Driver* magazine

Did you know?

- The car came with a host of options including color-coordinated trash cans.
- The GTO Judge could accelerate from 0-60 in 6.2 seconds.
- An original ragtop GTO Judge would now be worth in the region of $50,000.

Post-it Note

P

Birthplace: St. Paul, MN

Originator: Art Fry

Hometown Now: St. Paul, MN

Date Introduced: 1980

Estimated Number of Post-it Notes So
 Since 1980: 1 trillion

Stock Exchange Symbol: MMM (3M)

3M Founded: 1902

3M Sales: $20 billion in 2004

In 1968, scientist Dr. Spencer Silver of 3M in St.
Paul, Minnesota, developed an adhesive whose
limited sticking power allowed objects coated
with it to be attached to other surfaces– and then
pulled away from them without causing damage.
In 1973, another chemist at 3M, Art Fry, came up
with an unexpected application for it. Fry, a member
of a church choir in St. Paul, was in the habit of
inserting slips of paper between the pages of his
hymnal to mark the position of the hymns to be
sung during a service. These had an infuriating
habit of falling out; but when he coated them
with the new adhesive, they
stayed in place and could be
peeled off easily. The 3M executives were not immediately
convinced by the notion of "sticky bookmarks," but eventually

Did you know?
- Post-it Notes are among the five biggest selling items of
  office stationery in America.
- 3M stands for Minnesota Mining and Manufacturing
  Company; it was founded in 1902.

Post-it Notes *"changed people's communication and organization behavior forever.*
3M Corporate Communication

decided to market "Post-it Notes" (as they were named) in 1980. The rest is history. A wide range of Post-its are now available. 3M also used the product to highlight special causes, such as "Super Sticky Notes" for the Breast Cancer Awareness campaign.

Q-Tips

Birthplace: New York, NY

Originator: Leo Gerstenzang

Hometown Now: New York City, NY

Date introduced: 1923

Original Product Name: Baby Gays

Number of Products: 15

Unit Cost Today: Between $0.01 and $0.04

Number of Q-Tips produced annually: 25.5 billion

Stock Exchange Symbol: UN

Leo Gerstenzang, a Polish émigré living in New York City, developed the first mass-produced cotton-tipped cleansing sticks as a safer, more convenient alternative to the improvised swabs, made from balls of cotton and toothpick stems, that he had seen his wife use on their newborn daughter. Manufactured by his own Leo Gerstenzang Infant Novelty Company, the new creations were initially known as 'Baby Gays', were renamed 'Q-Tips Baby Gays' in 1926, and ultimately, simply 'Q-Tips' (the 'Q' stands for 'quality'). Though originally conceived as a child-care product, customers soon found numerous other applications for Q-Tips, and by the late 1940s, demand was so high that a new factory in Long Island had to be opened to make them. Q-Tips are now commonly used for make-up application, delicate cleaning jobs and even craftwork and painting. Indeed, some doctors now advise against using Q-Tips for their

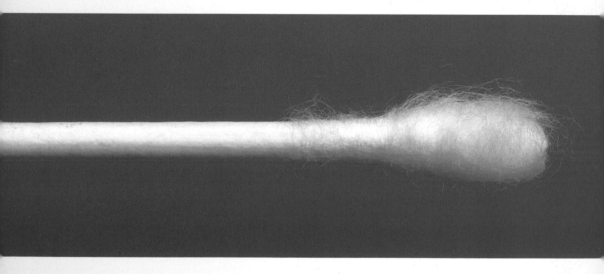

> **"Q-Tips cotton swabs are the ultimate beauty tool."**
> Mally Roncal, make-up artist

original function of cleaning inside the ear. Various improvements have been made to their design over the years: the tips have been made from pure cotton since the 1980s, and antibacterial Q-Tips were introduced in 1998. Unilever, who also own Ben & Jerry's, Dove, Hellman's, Knorr, Lipton, Popsicle, Skippy, Snuggle, and Vaseline, now owns the Q-Tips brand.

Did you know?

- The Q-Tip's inventor, Leo Gerstenzang, has a science library named after him at Brandeis University, Waltham, MA.
- Q-Tips are perennially popular items in the care packages sent to US troops stationed overseas.

R Radio Flyer Wagon

Birthplace: Chicago, IL

Originator: Antonio Pasin

Hometown Now: Chicago, IL

Date Introduced: 1917

Spokespeople: Robert and Paul Pasin

Original Price: $2.79 for original Radio Flyer

Number of Products: 5 steel and wood wagons

WWII Production: U.S. Army gas cans

Sixteen year-old Antonio Pasin emigrated from Italy with his parents in 1917. Arriving in Chicago, he struggled to find work, even though he was a skilled cabinetmaker, and ended up working for a sewer digging crew. But he never lost sight of his American dream, and invested in some used woodworking equipment. He used this to make wagons by night, which he sold by day. Pasin's first wagons were named "Liberty Coasters" in honor of the statue that had welcomed his family to their new country. The business grew, and by 1923, he had several employees.

Pasin was inspired by the mass-production techniques of the automotive industry to make a new metal wagon from pressed steel. Pasin called this the "Radio Flyer" in honor of two great products of the '30s: Marconi's radio, and the airplane. Even during the Depression, Americans tried to buy toys for their children, and the company continued to grow. Wagon production was suspended between 1942 and 1945, while the company manufactured steel cans for the armed services. Production resumed after the war, and baby boomers loved the Radio Flyer, which was now an American classic.

Over the years, the company has continued to add to its toy range, and has also brought out products for adults, such as garden carts and "Ski Sleds." The Radio Flyer itself has continued to develop, and the all-terrain Quad-Shock Wagon, complete with Monroe shock absorbers, is its latest incarnation.

"From the original Liberty Coaster Wagon at the turn of the century to the popular All-Terrain wagons of today, the 'little red wagon' has both inspired dreams and nurtured the wonders of childhood."

Robert and Paul Pasin, company owners

Did you know?

- In the '50s, Radio Flyer built a special blue wagon for members of Disney's Mickey Mouse Club.
- They also built a special yellow wagon to commemorate Disney's *Davy Crockett*.
- Radio Flyer is now run by Antonio Pasin's grandsons, Robert and Paul.

Ralph Lauren Oxford Shirt

R

Birthplace: New York City, NY	Date Introduced: 1967
Originator: Ralph Lauren	Number of Products: 28 Polo Ralph
Hometown Now: New York City, NY	Lauren formal shirts
Commentator: Paul Goldberg, *New York*	Revenue: 2004 corporate world sales
Times	of $4.8 billion

Ralph Lauren started his own company in 1967 with a range of men's neckwear, funded by a $50,000 loan. Completely bucking the trend, his handmade Polo ties were wide and made from opulent materials, but were immediately successful. But Ralph Lauren has never been simply a fashion designer. From the very beginnings of his company, he has been purveying a way of life rather than just merchandise, and has been distilling American style for nearly forty years. His style of clothes

Did you know?

- Ralph Lauren was born Ralph Lifshitz into a middle-class Jewish family from The Bronx.
- Lauren has been happily married for 35 years, is a father of three, and has an estimated net worth of $1 billion.
- *Friends* character Rachel worked at Ralph Lauren until she was fired for going to a job interview with Gucci.
- A classic Ralph Lauren formal shirt currently retails for around $69.50.

> "Lauren has become a kind of one-man Bauhaus, a producer of everything from fabrics to furniture to buildings, all of which... form... a fully designed life."
>
> Paul Goldberg, *New York Times*

for both men and women is a synthesis of American influences and European tailoring. It has also been his intention to avoid transient fashion, and to evolve a recognizably "Lauren" look. As he himself says, "I never went to fashion school (in fact, he studied business at City College in Manhattan) – I was a young guy who had some style."

Designing costumes for *Gatsby* and *Annie Hall* in the mid-'70s showcased his style to a far wider audience, and Robert Redford, Mia Farrow, and Diane Keaton were the most fantastic models for the Lauren look. But Lauren has become far more than a clothes retailer. He launched an instantly recognizable range of home wear in 1983, and opened the RL Restaurant in 1999. The designer's flagship store in Madison Avenue's Rhinelander Mansion is the epitome of the Ralph Lauren look: a fusion of antique, vintage, and contemporary influences.

Ray-Ban Wayfarers

R

Established: 1937

Hometown now: Port Washington, NY

Wayfarers Introduced: 1952

Today's Price: From $79

Number of Products: 9 plus Wayfarers

Current Owners: Luxottica Group
  (acquired Ray-Ban in 1999)

Luxottica Earnings First quarter 2005:
  €1.04 billion

Stock Exchange Symbol: LUX

Ray-Ban is the best-selling brand of sunglasses in the world. The company sold 10,000,000 pairs in 1998. An all-American product, Ray-Ban was established as a manufacturing brand in 1937, following the invention of the anti-glare Aviator range in 1936. These sunglasses were developed in conjunction with the U.S. Air Force, to increase flier safety. Ray-Ban introduced the iconic Wayfarer model in 1952, and its flattering lines and legendary sun performance ensured that it would be hugely popular with ordinary Americans and celebrities alike. In fact, the list of famous people to wear this model is extraordinary. It includes such luminaries as Audrey Hepburn, Ray Charles, Bob Dylan, The Blues Brothers, Roy Orbison, Mike Jagger, and Leonardo DiCaprio. The original Wayfarers spawned a succession of descendants, and Wayfarer II versions are now available in both small and large sizes, and with polarized lenses.

Luxottica acquired the brand in 1999, and Ray-Ban became the most successful partner in an extensive range of designer eyewear. Despite the trend towards more expensive designer sunglasses, middle-priced Ray-Bans have maintained their pre-eminent market position.

*"Every field has its Connoisseur's Choice.
For British Invasion bands, it's the Kinks.
For sunglasses it's Ray-Ban Wayfarers."*
David Wondrich, *Esquire*

Did you know?

- When Tom Cruise wore a pair of 1952 Wayfarers in *Risky Business*, he took annual Wayfarer sales from 18,000 to 260,000 in 1983.
- Another Tom Cruise blockbuster, *Top Gun* did the same for Ray-Ban Aviators.
- Ray-Bans are the best-selling sunglasses in the world.

Revell Model Kits

R

Birthplace: Venice, CA	**Today's Price:** $49.95 Make 'N Take
Originator: Lewis Glasser	Event Package
Hometown Now: Northbrook, IL	**Models for Ages:** 8 plus
Date Introduced: 1943	**Skill Levels:** Easy Snap to Advance
Revell Germany: 1957	Gluing

Lewis Glasser started Revell in the '40s, but the real golden age of modeling was in the '60s and '70s. Many of these kids returned to the hobby as adults. Revell had some of its first successes with iconic models like their "Cutty Sark" and American car kits. Their distinctive Jack Leynwood box artwork helped them to develop a growing cult following. Revell also grew through acquisition, buying Monogram for their excellent line of model airplanes. Today, the company concentrates on plastic kits, but also offers some die-cast models. Revell's new releases echo Detroit's hot new products, including the 2006 Mustang GT and March 839 Blue Thunder.

Did you know?
- The company name is now humorously shortened to "Revellogram."
- Revell re-imports the products of its German subsidiary company.
- Lewis Glasser boasted that he never made a Revell kit.

Rollerblades

R

Birthplace: Minneapolis, MN

Originators: Scott and Brennan Olson

Hometown Now: Bordentown, NY

Date Introduced: 1980

Number of Products: 17 models

Today's Price: $349 for Rollerblade
Lightning 10-speed skates

Billion Dollar Industry: by 1997

Other Manufacturers: Ultra Wheels,
Oxygen, K2

First, there came roller skating, then there came rollerblading. The hockey-playing Olson brothers discovered an antique pair of roller skates with an "in-line" wheel arrangement. These had been invented by James Plimpton in 1863. They took the basic design as the inspiration behind their Rollerblades, adding polyurethane wheels, ice hockey boots and a rubber toe-brake. They formed Rollerblade Inc. in 1980. Their brand became a synonym for the sport. The brothers soon sold out and the new owners launched the first, massively successful Rollerblade, the Lightning TRS. Over twenty companies now manufacture the skates. Americans of all ages now rollerblade—for fun, fitness or speed.

Did you know?

- More than 26 million Americans rollerblade.
- Rollerblading burns as many calories as running.

Roller Coaster

R

Birthplace: Coney Island, NY

Originator: La Marcus Adna Thompson

Hometown Now: Coney Island, NY

Date Introduced: 1884

Spokesperson: John Wardley

Switchback Railway Ride Price: $0.10

Cyclone Designer: Vernon Keenan

Ride Price: $0.25

Original Cost: $100,000

Date Opened: 1927

The "Father of the American Roller Coaster," La Marcus Thompson, was always creative. He made a butter churn for his mother and an ox-cart for his father before turning his hand to roller coasters. In the 1880s , Coney Island was shaping up to become the first amusement park in America. It was there in 1884 that Thompson built his first roller coaster, the Switchback Railway. It was a huge success even at 10 cents a ride. The name is no coincidence, as many early claimants to the title of "forefather" to the roller coaster were actually scenic railways, like the one at Mauch Chunk, Pennsylvania. But by the '20s, the Coney Island Park was due an update. Older rides like the Giant Racer, built in 1911, were torn down to make way for new generations of thrill rides. The Cyclone became the ride by which other rides were rated. Designed by Vernon Keenan and built by the Harry C. Baker Company, it opened on June 26, 1927. Nearly 80 years later, the Cyclone survives as one of the oldest working examples of a classic wooden roller coaster.

Did you know?

- The name "roller coaster" came from an amusement park in Haverhill, Massachusetts, where the sleds ran on a track of wooden rollers.
- Chris Feucht, another notable roller coaster designer, added lap bars to secure passengers in the 1930s.

Cyclone Specifications
Height: 85 feet

Max Drop: 85 feet

Top Speed: 60 mph

Length: 2,640 feet

"There is no doubt that there is a place in society for providing fun and thrills that are exhilarating and where there is a perceived sense of danger."

John Wardley, Coaster Designer

S Sawzall

Birthplace: Milwaukee, WI	Sawzall Introduced: 1951
Company Founder: A. F. Seibert	Milwaukee Products: Over 500
Originators: Jerome L. Schnetter and	Warranty Period: 5 years
Edward W. Ristow	Stock Exchange Symbol: TTI
Hometown Now: Brookfield, WI	(Techtronic Industries)

A. H. Petersen designed and supplied Henry Ford with the first lightweight, one-handed drill, "The Hole Shooter" for his famous assembly line. A. F. Seibert joined him in 1922, and bought out Petersen to form The Milwaukee Electric Tool Corporation in 1924. Part of the business was repairing other power tool products, and Milwaukee soon became aware of the design faults and problems of their competitors. They used this opportunity to design and incorporate improvements in their own products, and succeeded in making their range the "industry standard." The company has always aimed its product at the trade user and their advertising slogan "designed by professionals for professionals" encapsulates this perfectly. When they launched the Sawzall in 1951, it revolutionized the tool market. With only three moving parts, its ¾ inch cutting stroke made it ideal for sawing and roughing out. Aimed at the professional market, where time really is money, the company's advertising emphasized that the cost of the tool would be saved on the first job. A collector's edition Super Sawzall was launched in 1999 to mark the seventy-fifth anniversary of the company.

> "Milwaukee's legendary Sawzall is the best-known tool associated with these men."
> *Tools Of The Trade Hall of Fame* nomination for Sawzall's Originators–Jerome L. Schnetter and Edward W. Ristow

Did you know?

- Seibert's company has now been in business for over 80 years.
- Over 3,500 accessories are available for Milwaukee power tools.
- Sawzall is cooperating with that other Milwaukee legend, Harley-Davidson, in the "Build a Bike" event of the 2005 Harley-Davidson Rally celebrations.
- Milwaukee publishes its own *Cool Gear* catalog, featuring apparel and accessories with the company logo.

S Schwinn Bicycles

Birthplace: Chicago, IL

Originator: Ignaz Schwinn

Hometown Now: Madison, WI

Date Company Started: October 22, 1895

Date Acquired By Present Owners: 2004

Today's Price Range: $109.99 to $3999.99

Brand Owners: Dorel Industries

Dorel CEO: Martin Schwartz

Sister Brands: GT Bicycles, Mongoose

The twenty-first century Fastback is a typical Schwinn, a bike packed with features and technology that looks the part. It has N'Litened tube sets, reflex carbon technology, and a rakish semi-sloping frame. Schwinn bicycles have always stood out from the pack.

Back in the '40s, the Schwinn Cruiser set the standard for Hollywood's portrayal of cycling chic, with its cantilever frame, swooping handlebars,

and no visible brake levers (stopping was effected by backpedal action). Like many Schwinn classics, an updated version of this model is still offered for sale in the catalog. The Schwinn Sting-Ray was a classic model from the '60s. It was a cool street bike, which (when suitably modified) provided the ideal machine for BMX-ing. This bike has also been recently relaunched, with the slogan "the rebirth of cool." Schwinn

Did you know?

- The Schwinn bike has been an American icon for over a century.
- The BMX craze can trace its roots back to the Schwinn Sting-Ray of the '60s.
- Pro Rider T. J. Levin does demos for Schwinn, and has a model named for him.

*"World class performance
on an economy class budget."*
Schwinn Fastback advertising slogan

remained family owned until 1993 when the company changed hands and moved from Chicago to Boulder, Colorado. It later merged with GT Cycles and was subsequently bought by distribution giant Pacific Cycle.

Dorel Industries, the company's present owners, subsequently acquired Pacific. Despite these changes in ownership, the Schwinn heritage has remained intact for over 100 years.

S   Scotch Tape

Birthplace: St. Paul, MN

Originator: 3M

Hometown Now: St. Paul, MN

Date Introduced: 1930

Original Name: Scotch Cellulose Tape

Today's Price: $1.46 (450-inch roll of Scotch Magic Transparent Tape)

Scotch Tape's U.S. Market Share: 90 percent

Stock Exchange Symbol: MMM

> *"You should have no hesitancy in equipping yourself to put this product on the market ....There will be a sufficient volume of sales to justify the expenditure."*
> Customer reaction to prototype roll of Scotch tape, 1930

Richard G. Drew (1899–1980) began working for 3M in St. Paul, Minnesota, in 1923. Two years later, he developed the first-ever masking tape for the company, and took a sample roll across town to an automobile paint shop for testing. Unfortunately, the prototype paper tape was insufficiently sticky, and when it failed to stay in place, an exasperated vehicle sprayer told Drew to return it to his "Scotch"—i.e. "cheap"—superiors and get them to add more adhesive! 3M subsequently adopted "Scotch" as a trademark; after the launch of the now stickier Scotch masking tape, Drew had the notion of coating cellophane with adhesive, and using it as an insulating material. This idea was eventually abandoned, but by mid-1930, Drew had produced a sticky, cellophane-backed tape that was waterproof, transparent, and intended for packaging. However, once the new product went on sale under the Scotch name that fall, customers found applications for it that had never been envisaged by its creators, and by the end of the 1930s it was already a household and office essential.

Did you know?

- The distinctive 3M Scotch tape dispenser, with its built-in cutter, was developed by one of Richard Drew's colleagues, John A. Borden, in 1932.
- Sales of Scotch tape in 1930 totaled a disappointing $33!
- The tape was originally supplied in blue and white packaging; 3M began using its now-familiar tartan motif in 1945.

S Scrabble

Birthplace: Poughkeepsie, NY

Originator: Alfred Mosher Butts

Hometown Now: Pawtucket, RI

Game Created: 1930s

Scrabble Launched: 1948

Original Price: $1.50

Today's Price: $14.45

Number of Products: 8 Scrabble games

Number Sold: 100,000,000 plus

Stock Exchange Symbol: HAS

When Alfred Mosher Butts (1899–1993) of Poughkeepsie, New York, lost his job as an architect during the Great Depression, he turned his attention to creating a salable word game. His first effort, Lexico, attracted no interest, and was denied a patent, although he managed to sell a few homemade sets at $1.50 apiece. Undaunted, he made some modifications, renamed the game Criss-Cross Words, and showed it to businessman James Brunot in 1939. War intervened, but in 1948, having suggested some

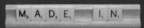

rule changes, and renamed it Scrabble, Brunot undertook to manufacture and market the game. Initial sales were poor; but Scrabble's fortunes changed dramatically after being "discovered" in 1952 by New York City's prestigious department store, Macy's. Hasbro estimate that one in every three American homes now possesses a set.

Did you know?

- U.S. Scrabble tournaments are organized by the National Scrabble Association, founded in 1978.
- Two million sets of the game are sold in America every year.
- Chambers offer an on-line Scrabble Wordchecker.

Sears, Roebuck Catalog

Birthplace: Chicago, IL

Originators: Richard W. Sears and
   Alvah C. Roebuck

Hometown Now: Hoffman Estates, IL

First General Catalog: 1896

Catalog Discontinued: 1993

Sales In 1892: $296,000

Sales in 1900: $10,600,000

Sales in 1945: $1 billion

Sales Now: $55 billion

Perhaps of all U.S. companies, Sears, **Roebuck and Company is the most responsible for stimulating the mass consumerism of the twentieth century.** Sears did this by bringing exciting new products right to America's doorstep. Back in the eighteenth century, rural general storekeepers were exploiting farmers by charging exorbitant prices for basic goods. Sears spotted a gap in the market, and their catalog opened the way for the company to become the one–time biggest corporation in the world. They opened their first retail store in 1925, and their 500th dealer store in 1997. For many Americans, Sears remains their retailer of choice.

Did you know?
- It was said that the Sears catalog was one of only two books read by rural Americans.
- Sears is now the leading home appliance retailer in the U.S.A.
- Sears continues to operate a modern form of "mail order" through Sears.com.

Sharpie Markers

S

Birthplace: Worcester, MS

Originators: Frederick W. Redington
  and William H. Sanford Jr.

Hometown Now: Bellwood, IL

Marker Introduced: 1964

Number of Products: 27 marker
  families, 18 tips

Sharpie Colours: 49

Number Sold: 200 million (by end
  2002)

The Sanford Manufacturing Company was founded in 1857 in Worcester, Mississippi, selling ink and glue. The company then moved to Chicago in 1866, but although it narrowly managed to escape the great Chicago fire, ironically the factory burned down in 1899. Nonetheless, the company survived and rebuilt its headquarters at its present location in Bellwood, Illinois. They introduced their first marker in 1964 and that single, signature product really took the company into another league. The original marker has evolved over the years and has become best-selling marker in the world. The $5 billion memorabilia market has been part of its success as autograph seekers and celebrities both use Sharpie markers.

Did you know?

• Sanford commissioned a Norman Rockwell painting in 1927 to commemorate their 70th anniversary.

• Sharpie is the sponsor of NASCAR's most popular event, the Sharpie 500.

Shure Microphones

S

Company Established: 1925

Originator: Sidney N. Shure

Hometown Now: Niles, IL

Original Business: radio parts
    wholesaler

SM58 Introduced: 1966

Today's Price for SM58: from $99.95

Weight of SM58: 10.5 oz

Number of Products: 5 performance
    microphones

Shure Brothers Inc. broke new ground with their **SM (studio microphone) 58, which appeared in 1966.** Despite its name, it is intended as much for live performance as recording wor. At its heart is the Unidyne III capsule, which the company's engineers had previously subjected to a barrage of extreme test that included a soaking in salt water in order to prove its resilience. The SM58 also boasts a spherical filter, mounted inside its outer grille. In the words of one early Shure advertisement, this guarded "against the effects of some singers' audio-degrading habit of 'mouthing' the microphone." Its ability to withstand abuse, combined with an audio response tailored to make voices sound their best, has made the SM58 a favorite with pop and rock vocalists. More than thirty years after its launch, it is still in daily use onstage and in the studio.

Did you know?
- It is used and endorsed by a long list of stars, including The Who's Roger Daltrey.
- The SM58 is the world's best-selling microphone.

S Silly Putty

Birthplace: New Haven, CT

Originator: James Wright

Hometown now: Easton, PA

Date Introduced: 1949

Original Price: $2

Today's Price: $1.99 for Original Egg

Number of Products: 10 packs

Number Sold: 300 million eggs plus

Owners: Binney & Smith

During the '40s, the interruption of rubber supplies from the Far East was hindering the War effort, so the U.S. government asked scientists to develop a formula for a synthetic rubber compound. General Electric scientist James Wright was working on this project when he accidentally invented "bouncing rubber" by combining boric acid and silicone oil. Ruth Fallgatter (the owner of the New Haven Block toy shop) and marketing consultant Peter Hodgson adopted the product, and offered it at $2. It was an instant hit. Peter Hodgson established a company manufacturing "bouncing rubber" in 1950, reduced the price to $1, launched the familiar egg packaging, and coined the instantly memorable product name.

Did you know?

- Silly Putty (packed in special sterling silver eggs) went around the moon with Apollo 8 in 1968.
- Peter Hodgson died in 1976, leaving an estate of $140 million.
- Therapists recommend Silly Putty for stress relief, and to help patients give up smoking.

"The Toy with one moving part."
Peter Hodgson, Silly Putty Manufacturer

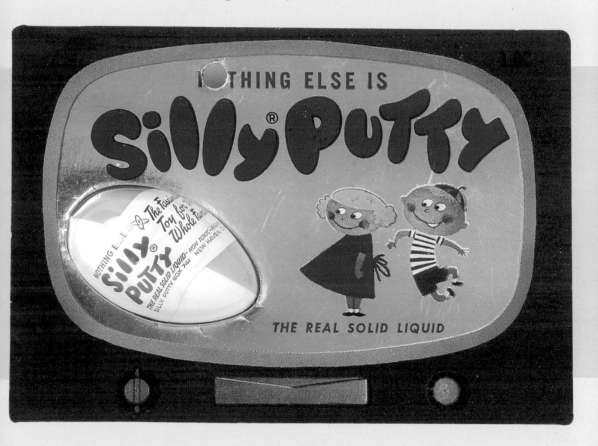

A favorable article in *The New Yorker* really launched the product, and orders for over 250,000 eggs flowed in. Advertising during *Howdy Doody* and *Captain Kangaroo* built on this success. Metallic Gold Silly Putty was introduced in 2000 to celebrate the golden anniversary of the toy, and a 14-carat gold egg was offered for the most inventive use of the product.

S | Skippy Peanut Butter

Birthplace: Alameda, CA

Originator: J. L. Rosefield

Hometown Now: Little Rock, AR

Date Introduced: 1933

First Crunchy Peanut Butter: 1934

Today's Price: $4.90

Annual U.S. Output: c. 10 million cases

Annual Global Sales: c. 90 million jars

Brand Owner: Unilever

Stock Exchange Symbol: UN

Peanut pastes started to appear in the 1890s and 1900s, but the thick, creamy spread we know today was created when Californian manufacturer J. L. Rosefield patented a process preventing the oil in the mixture from separating. Rosefield's company began producing Skippy peanut butter at its Alameda factory in 1933; the "Skippy" name had previously been associated with a popular comic strip character. The product soon became a national favorite, and its nutritious qualities made it an important staple during World War II when large numbers of jars were shipped to Hawaii to alleviate shortages of high-protein foods there. Radio- and TV-sponsored shows sustained Skippy's post-war popularity, and in 1955 the brand was acquired by Best Foods, which is now owned by Unilever. All of the U.S.A.'s Skippy peanut butter is now made at a 158,000-sq.-ft. plant in Little Rock, Arkansas.

Did you know?

- The average American child will eat 1,500 peanut butter sandwiches by the time they graduate high school.
- The U.S. peanut butter market is worth some $800 million a year.
- Botanically speaking, the peanut is not a nut but a "legume."

Slinky

S

Birthplace: Philadelphia, PA

Originators: Richard and Betty James

Hometown Now: Hollidaysburg, PA

Date Introduced: 1945

Date Patented: November 1, 1945

Original Price: $1

Today's Price: $3.49

Number Sold: 300,000,000 plus

Length of a Slinky: 80 feet

Current Manufacturer: Poof-Slinky, Inc.

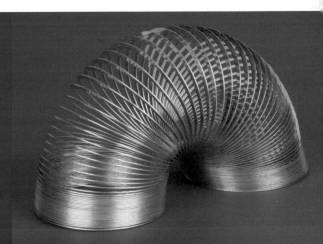

In 1943, mechanical engineer Richard James was aboard a U.S. Navy ship, testing spring-based devices intended to keep the vessel's instruments steady at sea. During the experiments, one of the coiled springs he was working with fell from a shelf—but then kept moving across the deck! Back at home in Philadelphia, James demonstrated the phenomenon to his wife, Betty, and by 1945, the couple had refined the "walking spring" into a toy that Mrs. James named "Slinky." They were unsure of its commercial potential, and were surprised and delighted when they sold 400 Slinkys in just 90 minutes at a local department store that November. Richard and Betty set up their own Philadelphia-based company to manufacture the unusual plaything; however, in 1961, following the breakup of their marriage, Mrs. James took over the business and moved it to Hollidaysburg, PA, where Slinkys have been made ever since.

Did you know?

- "It's fun for a girl and a boy" was the '70s slogan.
- In 2001, following a downturn in sales, Slinky CEO Bob Rollins wittily commented: "We'll bounce back no matter how far you stretch us."
- In 2002, Slinky became the Official State Toy of Pennsylvania.

Smith & Wesson .44 Magnum

Birthplace: Springfield, MA

Originator: Daniel B. Wesson

Hometown: Springfield, MA

Date Introduced: 1955

Spokesperson: Inspector Harry Callahan

Today's Price: $400

Number of Products: 4 models in the series

Number Sold: 800,000

Stock Exchange symbol: SWB

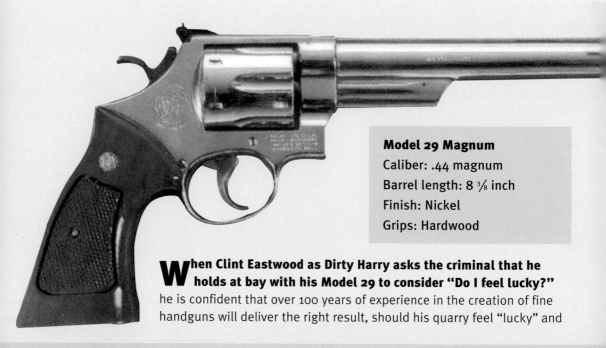

Model 29 Magnum
Caliber: .44 magnum
Barrel length: 8 ³⁄₈ inch
Finish: Nickel
Grips: Hardwood

When Clint Eastwood as Dirty Harry asks the criminal that he holds at bay with his Model 29 to consider "Do I feel lucky?" he is confident that over 100 years of experience in the creation of fine handguns will deliver the right result, should his quarry feel "lucky" and

Did you know?

- The sales boost created by the gun's starring role in *Dirty Harry* caused a five-year sales surge.
- Buffalo Bill killed a buffalo at 30 yards with a forerunner of the gun.

> *"I know what you're thinking. Did he fire six shots or only five? Well to tell you the truth, in all this excitement I kind of lost track myself. But being as this is a .44 Magnum, the most powerful handgun in the world, and would blow your head clean off, you've got to ask yourself a question: Do I feel lucky? Well do ya, punk?"*
>
> Harry Callahan, *Dirty Harry*

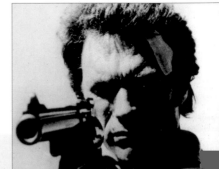

make a run for it. When Horace Smith and Daniel Wesson combined their gun-making skills in the middle of the nineteenth century, they must have scarcely dreamed that they were originating a brand that would become synonymous with robust and powerful handguns. However, we know from the company history that Smith and Wesson guns were not employed exclusively on the right side of the law. A selection of miscreants used a distant forebear of the Model 29, the No. 3, including Jesse and Frank James, Cole Younger, and his lady friend Belle Starr (AKA "The Bandit Queen"). The company opened its plant in Springfield, Massachusetts, in 1858 and was so successful that by the mid-1860s the founders paid themselves a handsome $160,000 a year each.

- Many owners are scared to fire their guns because of the loud report and violent recoil.
- Dan Wesson had to elope with his intended wife, Cynthia Hawes, because her father objected to her marrying an itinerant gunsmith.

S Snickers

Birthplace: Chicago, IL	Original Price: $0.05
Originator: Frank C. Mars	Today's Price: $0.75
Hometown Now: Hackettstown, NJ	Number of Products: 5
Date Introduced: 1930 (chocolate version)	Annual Global Sales Revenues for Snickers: $2 billion

The first Snickers bar, with a peanut filling but no chocolate, made its debut in 1923; it was not until seven years later that candy maker Frank C. Mars began producing the now-familiar version at his new plant in Chicago. The snack, named after the Mars family's horse, has gone on to become America's biggest-selling candy bar. For many years, Snickers was known as "Marathon" in Britain, though the labeling was changed there in the early 1990s, and the "Marathon" brand is now used solely for the vitamin-enriched "energy" versions of Snickers introduced in 2003. Demand for both new and regular Snickers bars remains strong, contributing substantially to Mars's $5 billion annual sales figures.

Did you know?

- Though Mars's HQ is in Hackettstown, New Jersey, Snickers bars are actually manufactured at plants in Chicago, Illinois, and Waco, Texas.
- Every Snickers bar contains about 16 peanuts; 99 tons of nuts are used every day during U.S. Snickers production.
- In 2004, the Mars Chicago factory celebrated its seventy-fifth anniversary. During the '40s, it pioneered the use of automatic wrapping machines for candy bars.

SPAM

Birthplace: Austin, MN

Originator: Hormel Foods

Hometown Now: Austin, MN

Date Introduced: 1937

SPAM Museum Opened: 2001

Original Price: $0.15 (24oz can)

Today's Price: $2.95 (12oz can)

Number of Products: 5

Number Sold: 6 billion plus

Stock Exchange Symbol: HRL

Hormel Foods launched its canned Spiced Ham in 1937. Shortly afterwards, a competition was held to find a better name for the product; the winner, actor Kenneth Daigneau, came up with "SPAM." Consumption of the pink luncheon meat soared during World War II, and by 1959, a billion cans had been sold worldwide. Though often mocked by humorists like Monty Python's Flying Circus (authors of the notorious "SPAM Song"), it is now a culinary institution, boasting a Fan Club and even a museum dedicated to its history.

Did you know?

- During World War II, SPAM had its own fighting mascot — "Slammin' Spammy," the bomb-throwing pig.
- SPAM is a contracted version of "spiced ham."
- A can of SPAM is consumed once every 3.1 seconds in the U.S.A.

Starbucks

S

Birthplace: Seattle, WA

Concept Originator: Howard Schultz

Hometown now: Seattle, WA

Commentator: Seth Hoffman, President, Tampa Bay Young Republicans

Date Introduced: 1971

2004 Revenue: $5.294 billion

Number of Products: 7 basic coffees, limitless variables

Starbucks is a true phenomenon, having mushroomed from just one Seattle cafe in 1971 to a company with 6,000 outlets in 30 countries worldwide. But there is a mixed reaction to their success. Some see Starbucks as the benign face of creeping globalization, a "McDonald's for the new media generation." But *Fortune* rates the company as the third most admired, and eleventh in their list of "100 Best Companies to Work For." Howard Shultz, who joined the company in 1982, was the inspiration behind

Did you know?

- According to a web clairvoyant, the "Oracle of Starbucks," the author's ordering preference indicates a "lame" personality.
- The name "Starbucks" comes from Herman Melville's whaling novel, *Moby Dick*.

Starbucks' expansion. His travels to Italy introduced him to the coffee culture of the *barista* (bar owner), and a variety of exciting brews. Starbucks expanded to offer a virtually unlimited selection of coffees, teas, and cold drinks. Despite the company's stated concern for the environment, the U.S. Department of Transportation has identified a gas-guzzling trend the "Starbucks Effect"–miles added to the daily commute by gourmet coffee–crazed Americans.

"For me, with Starbucks, it's not what's on the cup, but what's in the cup."
Seth Hoffman commenting on "The Way I See It" campaign to put thought-provoking quotes on Starbuck's cups

S Steinway Pianos

Birthplace: New York, NY

Originator: Henry Engelhard Steinway

Hometown Now: Long Island City, NY

Date Founded: 1853

Price of First Steinway: $500

Home of First Steinway: Metropolitan Museum, NY

Annual Piano Output: 5,000

Value of Steinway Piano Bank: $15 million plus

Henry Engelhard Steinway was one of many German immigrants to New York. An accomplished cabinetmaker, he had already constructed 482 pianos in his native town of Seesen, Germany. His 483rd instrument was constructed in his Varick Street, Manhattan, loft and was sold to a New York family for $500. Still at home in its native city, this priceless piano now resides in the Metropolitan Museum of Art. Steinway's pianos gained virtually instant recognition, for their beauty and crafts-manship, and the company flourished.

In 1866, the Steinways opened New York's Steinway Hall, a 2,000-seat auditorium. In 1870, William Steinway bought 400 acres of farmland in Astoria, Queens, to build a larger factory. This area gradually became known as the "Steinway Settlement," and was a fully functioning village established for the company's workforce. The company was run by several generations of the Steinway family, who were a constant force behind its technical and design innovations. It is now publicly quoted and parent company Steinway Musical Instruments Inc. is the world's leading manufacturer of a wide range of musical instruments.

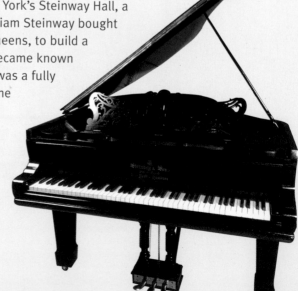

"With a tone so rich, I would never be afraid of the dark. Steinway is the only and the best!"

Harry Connick, Jr.

Did you know?

- According to *Forbes* magazine, the retail value of a Steinway concert grand has appreciated 200% in the past 10 years.
- Over 1,300 prominent artists worldwide have been designated "Steinway Artists."
- No artists are ever paid to endorse Steinway products.
- Steinway is running a sweepstakes to celebrate Mozart's 250th birthday with the prize as a trip to his birthplace of Salzburg, Austria.
- Several conservatories, colleges, and universities operate an "All-Steinway" policy.

S Stetson

Birthplace: Philadelphia, PA

Originator: John B. Stetson

Hometown Now: Garland, TX

Dated Introduced: 1865

Today's Price: $78–$218

Number of Products: Western hats, dress hats, caps

Number Sold: Millions

Stetson is owned by Hatco Inc. of Garland, TX

The Stetson is as Western as a chuck wagon and as manly as a cowboy. The hat was designed as a practical accessory but has become a subliminal icon of American manhood, worn by Presidents and ordinary Americans alike.

John B. Stetson caught TB during the 1860s, and moved south for the clear dry air of the Texas plains. He designed the

Did you know?

- The arrival of the Stetson spelled the end of the Mexican sombrero as standard cowboy apparel.
- Cowboys used the hats as wash bowls, and Stetsons were sometimes sized by the amount of water they could carry in the crown.
- President Bush was often seen wearing a Stetson during the Iraq War.

Stetson for the local cowboys, to protect them from the sun, heat, rain, hail, and snow. It could even be used to scoop a hatful of water. Stetson started to manufacture the new hat in 1865, with $100 capital and by 1866 the "Boss of the Plains" was already established as the "Hat of the West" and became the only branded American headwear that is universally recognized to this day.

Stetson died in 1906, but the hats are still made in Garland, Texas, in hundreds of different styles and colors, with the original classic styling and premium quality.

Sun-Maid Raisins

S

Birthplace: Fresno, CA

Originated by: Cooperative of
raisin growers

Hometown now: Kingsburg, CA

Date Introduced: 1912

First Sun-Maid Girl: Lorraine Collett

Today's Price: $2.55 (15oz carton)

Products: Raisins and currants

**1 pound of Raisins = 4 pounds of fresh
grapes**

America's favorite dried fruit has its
origins in the first grape vines planted
in California back in the late 1700s. In 1912,
a group of raisin growers formed the California
Associated Raisin Company. Their *raison d'etre*
was to promote the consumption of raisins and
to promote the fruit. They chose the brand
name "Sun-Maid" in order to reflect the fact
that the raisins were dried naturally on the vine.
The first Sun-Maid girl was appointed in 1915,
complete with her famous red bonnet. By 1918,
85% of the California raisin growers had joined
the cooperative. The Sun-Maid factory now
covers 130 acres, and 75% of the raisins used
by the company are grown within 25 miles of
the plant.

Did you know?

- Sun-Maid is the world's number one brand of raisins.
- The first Sun-Maid girl flew over San Francisco, dropping raisins.
- Sun-Maid raisins are made up from three grape varieties, 97% Thompson
  Seedless, 2% Zante currants and 1% Muscat.

S   Super Glue

Birthplace: Rochester, NY

Originator: Harry Coover

Employer: Eastman Kodak

Date Invented: 1942

Original Compound: Eastman 910

Patent Number: 2,768,109

Product Launched: 1958

Today's Price: Approx. $2.99 (½oz)

Other Brand-names: Loctite, Krazy
  Glue, Flash

Like so many brilliant inventions, Super Glue was discovered by accident. Harry Coover and his team were searching for a formula for an optically clear plastic to make gun-

Did you know?

- Super Glue can withstand a ton of pressure applied to a one-square-inch bond.
- "Inadvertent self-administration of Super Glue" is a recognized medical phenomenon.
- Strange uses for Super Glue have inspired a large number of urban legends.

sights. This was during WWII, when so many scientists' activities were focused on the needs of the U.S. armed forces. It wasn't until the late '50s that the commercial potential of the product was realized, and the Super Glue product was launched. During his career, Harry Coover was awarded 460 patents, wrote over 60 academic papers, and was inducted into the National Inventors' Hall of Fame in 2004 at it's headquarters in Akron, Ohio.

Swingline Stapler

S

Company Established: 1931

Founder: Jack Linsky

Original Name: Parrot Speed Fastener Co.

Babe Stapler Introduced: 1934

Hometown Now: Lincolnshire, IL

Number of Products: 30 "everyday" staplers

Parent Company: Fortune Brands

Won: 5 Chicago Athenaeum "Good Design" Awards in 2004

The origins of the stapler are somewhat disputed, but it is thought to have been around in one form or another for around three hundred years. It is generally agreed that Charles H. Gould invented the modern stapler in 1868, and the B. Jahn Manufacturing Company took his innovation a stage further by producing the first strip of staples. But Swingline revolutionized the stapling process in the late '30s by introducing a stapler that opened at the top to accept the staple strip with ease. Before this, each staple has to

Did you know?

- Swingline's early motto was "Where Tradition and Innovation Are One."
- The first stapler to carry the Swingline name was launched in 1937.
- Swingline introduced the first electric stapler in 1956.

be inserted individually. A huge range of staplers is now available for home and office use, both electronic and hand-powered. Swingline's modern selection of staplers is now lighter, more powerful, ergonomic, and aesthetically pleasing. In 2002, the company launched the E-Z Use Stapler, which is specifically targeted to teens and is made in vivid color combinations and with soft-grip features.

T

Tabasco

Birthplace: Avery Island, LA

Originator: Edmund McIlhenny

Hometown Now: Avery Island, LA

Date Introduced: 1868

Today's Price: $1.10 per 2oz bottle

Spokesperson: Mr. Broussard, Tabasco official historian

Number of Products: 5 pepper sauces, "from mild to scorchin'"

Daily Production: 600,000 2oz bottles

According to McIlhenny family tradition, Edmund **"Mr. Ned" McIlhenny was on his way home after the Civil War when he met a traveller from South America.** He obtained some hot pepper seeds from the man, which he planted at his home on Avery Island the highest of five salt dome islands in the Louisiana swamps. McIlhenny then experimented with various pepper sauce recipes until he hit upon one he liked. The sauce was immediately successful in New York City, and its fame spread countrywide. Tabasco is made by the same method to this day. The peppers are harvested by hand when they are a bright, fiery red, mixed with Avery Island salt to produce pepper mash, fermented in white oak barrels for three years, and then blended with other ingredients to make the famous sauce. Tabasco is popular in many cocktails, including the Bloody Mary.

Did you know?

• The average consumer uses one 2oz bottle per year.

• Each 2oz bottles contains at least 720 drops of pepper sauce.

Teddy Bear

Birthplace: Brooklyn, NY

Originator: Morris Michtom

Location of Original Bear:
Smithsonian Institute,
Washington, DC

Date Introduced: 1902

Spokesperson: Theodore Roosevelt

Height of Original Bear: 21 inches

First Manufacturer: Ideal Novelty &
Toy Company, Brooklyn, NY

Although there had been stuffed bear toys before, the creation of the uniquely American "Teddy," a jointed, mohair pile bear, dates from 1902. Russian immigrant Morris Michtom ran a candy store in Brooklyn, which he decorated with cuddly toys sewn by his wife, Rose. Michtom was captivated by a cartoon in the *Washington Evening Post*, showing President Theodore Roosevelt refusing to shoot a tethered bear cub, and he persuaded Rose to sew a cuddly baby bear. Morris wrote to Roosevelt, asking if he could name the bear in his honor, and the President graciously agreed. The first true "teddy" was born.

Did you know?
- Germany's famous Steiff bear was introduced at the Leipzig Toy Fair of 1903.
- The teddy was immortalized by W.J. Bratton's song, "Teddy Bears' Picnic."
- "I don't believe that my name will do much for the image of your stuffed bear" President Roosevelt replied to Michtom's letter.

Texas Instruments Calculator

T

Birthplace: Dallas, TX

Originators: Jack Kilby, Jerry Merryman, and James Van Tassel

Prototype Developed: 1967

Calculator Patented: 1974

Hometown Now: Dallas, TX

Today's Price: Basic TI calculators are available from under $7.00

TI's Revenue for 2004: $12.5 billion

Stock Exchange Symbol: TXN

In 1967, a team of scientists at Texas Instruments, led by Jack Kilby, developed a prototype hand-held calculator using the microchip technology that Kilby himself had invented nine years before. It had no built-in display (a thermal printer was used instead), weighed almost 3 pounds, and measured about 4" by 6" by 1.75", but was substantially smaller and lighter than any of its predecessors, and was later awarded a patent. Though the device (named the "Caltech") never went into production, its circuitry was used, in a modified form, in the "Pocketronic" calculator introduced in 1970 by the Canon company in association with Texas Instruments. TI itself produced its first consumer-targeted calculator, the TI-2500, in 1972; it boasted an LED display, and sold for just under $120.

Did you know?

- In the mid-1960s, most electronic calculators were restricted to basic arithmetic, and were very expensive: one Japanese model cost $2,500.
- Jack Kilby, its inventor, is a Nobel Prize winner, and holds over 60 U.S. patents.
- The original TI prototype calculator is in the Smithsonian Institution.

Timberland Boots

T

Birthplace: Boston, MA

Originator: Nathan Swartz

Hometown Now: Stratham, NH

Timberland Name Introduced: 1973

Spokesperson: William F. Buckley Jr.

Target Age Range: 16–35

Today's Price: $130 (waterproof wheat nubuck men's 6" premium boot)

Revenue in 2003: $1.3 billion

Stock Exchange Symbol: TBL

Timberland has its origins in the Abington Shoe Company of Boston, Massachusetts, where Russian émigré Nathan Swartz was apprenticed as a bootmaker in 1918. By 1955, he had risen through the ranks to take control of the business, and over the following years he worked with his sons Herman and Sidney to produce footwear for various other manufacturers. Ten years later, the firm pioneered a method of making waterproof boots using injection molding instead of conventional stitching; these were labelled "Timberland" in 1973, and in 1978 the company itself adopted the same name. Since then, it has become famous not only for its boots and shoes, but also for its stylish leisure wear and accessories.

Did you know?

- Timberland is now run by Jeff Swartz, the grandson of its founder Nathan.
- Timberland fans include columnist William F. Buckley Jr., who once proclaimed them "the world's most comfortable shoe."
- "Timbs" are also the favorite footwear of many rap and hip-hop stars.

Times Square

T

Location: Broadway, 7th Avenue &
42nd Street, New York, NY

Named: April 8, 1904

Daily Number of Pedestrians Passing
Through the Square: 1.5 million

Annual Number of Tourists: 26 million
(recorded in 2002)

Number of Businesses: 5,000

Times Square's Nickname: "The
Crossroads of the World"

In 1904, the *New York Times* moved to new midtown Manhattan premises on Longacre Square—which, by April that year, had been renamed "Times Square" by Mayor George McClellan. The paper marked the change by throwing a street party outside the building on December 31, 1904, establishing the now-familiar tradition of New Year's Eve celebrations there. The area around the Square, already famous for its restaurants, soon developed into the city's principal theater and cinema district, and became a prime site for billboards and illuminated ads, earning its nickname, "The Great White Way." Sadly, by the '70s and '80s, a culture of sleaze and crime had taken hold there, though in more recent years, new legislation and massive investment have succeeded in restoring the Square's luster.

Did you know?

- 1907 saw the first lowering of the now-famous illuminated New Year's Eve Ball in Times Square.
- Public drinking was banned from Times Square New Year's Eve gatherings by Mayor Giuliani in 1994.
- The 37-foot-high NASDAQ sign in the Square cost over $37 million to install.

"When the New York Times [building] shall be completed… why would it not be fitting that the space about [it] be called 'Times Square'?"
J.W.C. Corbusier, letter to the *New York Times*, March 17, 1904

Timex Watches

Birthplace: Waterbury, CT

Originator: Waterbury Watch Co.

Hometown Now: Middlebury, CT

Original Price: $1 for Yankee pocket
   watch in 1900

Date Introduced: 1957

Today's Price: $71.99 for Ironman
   Data Link

Number Sold: One out of every three
   watches in the U.S.

The original Timex company of Waterbury Watch
was incorporated in the 1850s, just as America was
beginning to use mass production techniques to produce
cheap and reliable watches. In 1917, the company was
the first to mass-produce wristwatches, ordered by the
U.S. Army. The Timex brand itself dates from the '50s,
when the company launched their completely sealed
watches. Although these couldn't be repaired, they were
dustproof, rugged, and could "Take a Licking and Keep
On Ticking!" Indiglo face
lighting was introduced in
1992, with GPS (global
satellite positioning) and
data link watches are now
available. In 1995, Fairchild
Publications named Timex
as America's favorite
accessory brand.

Waterproof*

Rain, perspiration, even immersion in water, won't affect Timex performan

Dustproof*

Unlike ordinary watches, Timex case-construction keeps out dust and di

Shock-Resista

Hard bumps and thumps won't impair rugged Timex! Takes a licking yet keeps on ti

Timex Marlin. Easy to read dial. Chrome bezel. Stainless steel back. $9 95

Sold With ONE-YEAR Guarantee

Timex Marlin. Sweep-second hand. Radialite dial. Chrome bezel. Stainless steel back. $11 95

Did you know?

- Mark Twain carried a Yankee dollar watch.
- Timex's hometown is in the Naugatuck Valley of
   Connecticut, the "Switzerland of America."

Titleist Golf Balls

T

Birthplace: Acushnet, MS

Originator: Acushnet Process Company

Hometown Now: Fairhaven, MS

Date Introduced: 1932

Today's Price: From $29.95/dozen

Number of Employees Worldwide: 5,000

Number of Products: 9 plus

Stock Exchange Symbol: FO
  (Fortune Brands)

Golf balls have been through several stages of evolution since the game was first invented in Scotland in the fourteenth century. The first ball was called the "featherie," a leather-covered ball stuffed with goose feathers. The next major advance was the gutta-percha ball in the mid-nineteenth century, followed by the hand-hammered gutta version and the rubber ball. The standards for modern golf balls were established in 1932, and this coincided with the beginning of Titleist's manufacturing career. Theirs soon became the best-selling golf balls in history, a position the company has since maintained by continual technological development. Improved versions of five Titleist models are being introduced in 2005, as the "Number 1 Ball in Golf" reinvents itself for a new generation of golfers.

Did you know?
- Titleist is the most popular ball on the professional golfer tours worldwide.
- Many professional players, including Ernie Els and Ben Curtis, use Titleist balls and equipment.
- Ernie Els won golf's richest prize in his native South Africa at his first event using the Titleist Pro VI.

T Tonka Toys

Birthplace: Mound, MN	Today's Price: Tonka Toughest Mighty
Originator: Mound Metalcraft Co.	Truck $24.95
Hometown now: Hasbro HQ,	Number of Products: 30 trucks plus
Pawtucket, RI	Number Sold: 250 million plus
Date Introduced: 1947	Stock Exchange Symbol: HAS

Just after WWII, six cash-strapped Minnesota teachers set up the Mound Metalcraft Company, and started to make gardening hand tools in the basement of the local schoolhouse. In 1947, they acquired a competing company (owned by Edward C. Streater), and went into steel toy production. Their first two models were a steam shovel and a clam shell crane. The toys sold over 37,000 units in their first year and manufacture of the garden implements was abandoned. Named after the nearby Lake Minnetonka, the new company was called "Tonka" – the Sioux word for "great". Semis, wreckers, dump trucks; fire trucks and forklifts were added to the original two lines. The company soon gained a reputation for durability and realism, together with keeping up with the changes in real-life vehicles. Pick-ups were added in 1955, Jeeps in 1962, and the yellow Mighty Dump Truck in 1964. The latter was to become the company's best

selling, most instantly recognizable and enduring product. In 1965, Tonka's advertising featured a six ton elephant standing on a five pound Mighty Dump Truck to demonstrate its durability. This is one of the most important aspects of the company's founding premise, of producing toys that would be long-lasting, reasonably priced, and fun. In 1991, Tonka was brought into the Hasbro stable of toys, with other iconic brands like Mr. Potato Head, Monopoly, and Play-Doh. In 2000, Tonka Trucks joined 30 other playtime luminaries in the National Toy Hall of Fame.

"Tonka is Big Fun!"
Hasbro

Did you know?
- Tonka uses more than 119,000 pounds of yellow paint in a year.
- The company uses 5.1 million pounds of sheet metal annually to produce its steel products.

Topps Baseball Cards

Birthplace: Brooklyn, NY

Originator: Sy Berger

Hometown Now: Manhattan, NY

Date Introduced: 1950

Original Price: $0.05

Collectors' Price Today: $10,000 plus

Number Of Brands: 12 plus

Company Revenue: $290,079,000

Number Employees: 420

Stock Exchange Symbol: TOPP

It is often said that America is a nation of collectors. Topps started out as a marketing aid to selling gum, but ended up as the main deal. Topps trading cards began in 1950, featuring Hopalong Cassidy, Frank Buck, and All-American Football. Baseball cards made a shaky entrance in 1951 but were quickly repackaged (in 1952) by knowledgeable Sy Berger into the cards we know today. The winning formula turned out to be a combination of a player image, team logo, vital statistics, and full playing record. The first set featured rookies Mickey Mantle and Willie Mays and is now very collectible indeed. You could even say that players' reputations were enhanced by Topps exposure. Cards from the '50s are now recognized as valuable pieces of Americana and are preserved by prestigious art museums. Parallel to their sport cards, Topps have also developed cards with their other original themes of entertainment and popular culture. These celebrated icons as diverse as John F. Kennedy, the Beatles, *Star Wars,* and Pokemon. In the true words of the company history: "You can count on Topps to be there with popular products for collectors the world over." The Topps vault was recently opened for the first time, and archive cards were made available to an avid audience of collectors. Topps collectors' stories tend to go like this: "My friend's brother bought Topps out of his allowance, every week for years, he never opened them but stashed them under his bed. One day he will sell them." What about the buyer? Will they open the packs?

> *"People have waited years and years to own something from the Topps Archives."*
> Warren Friss, director, Topps Archive

Did you Know?

- The Andy Pafko card from the first baseball set (1952) is by far the most valuable. Being the top card in the pack meant that these often suffered devastating rubber band damage.
- Topps Vault treasures are being sold through a special arrangement with eBay.
- Topps cards have been inducted into The Baseball Hall of Fame.

Traffic Lights

T

Inventor: Superintendent William
  L. Potts

First three-color Location: Detroit, MI

Date Introduced: 1920 (originally they
  were manually controlled)

First electrically synchronized traffic
  lights: 1924

Location: New York City, NY

Bronze Traffic Towers: $28,000 each

No. of traffic signals today: 330,000

African-American Garrett Morgan is credited **with the invention of the first traffic signal. It was a T-shaped pole unit with three command positions,** Stop, Go, and Halt all traffic (in favor of pedestrians). The American Traffic Signal Company developed this idea, and introduced the first red/green electrical traffic signal to Cleveland, Ohio in 1914 (based on James Hoge's invention). Detroit policeman William Potts took this idea a stage further, introducing the third yellow light to his signals, which were mounted atop traffic towers. The police controlled these manually. One of these original towers is exhibited at the Henry Ford Museum in Dearborn, and is clearly recognizable as the forerunner of the modern signals we know today.

Did you know?

- James Hoge's design, as manufactured by the American Traffic Signal Company, also had a buzzer to warn of color changes.

Tupperware

T

Originator: Earl Silas Tupper

Tupper's Birthplace: Berlin, NH

Hometown Now: Orlando, FL

Date Introduced: 1947

Today's Price: $10–$275

Number of Products: 100s!

Annual Sales: $1.2 billion plus

Company Selling Price: $ 16 million
 in 1958

Stock Exchange Symbol: TUP

Earl Silas Tupper (1908–1983) was a New Hampshire tree surgeon who started work for DuPont when the Great Depression drove him out of business. He became fascinated by plastics, and experimented with polyethylene in his spare time. His experimentation led to his founding of the Tupperware Plastics Company in 1938, and his patent for the Tupperware seal in 1947. But customers were initially unenthused by the product.

Did you know?

- A Tupperware demonstration starts every 2 seconds, somewhere in the world.
- The product was originally called Wonderbowl.
- At least 90% of American households own at least one piece of Tupperware.
- Tupperware was featured by the Museum of Modern Art in 1956.

It was only when Tupper's business associate, divorcée Brownie Wise, invented the Tupperware Party that sales really took off. Post-war America was in love with convenience, and Tupperware demonstrations helped the customers to understand the product. Direct home selling was so successful that Tupper removed his product from ordinary stores in 1951. His "Tupperware Ladies" became a social phenomenon empowering women to develop their own lucrative careers.

TV Dinners

T

Birthplace: Omaha, Nebraska

Originator: Gerry Thomas

Hometown now: Allentown, PA

Date Introduced: 1953

Original Price: $0.98

Number of Products: 76 Swanson
   dinner varieties

Number Sold: 10+ million in first year

Swanson owned by Pinnacle Foods
   Corporation

Gerry Thomas invented both the product and name of the Swanson TV dinner, "The King of Convenience Foods." Ironically, it is said that the invention was in response to the need to dispose of 270 tons of left over Thanksgiving turkey.
The idea for the tray came from airline food service, while the product name reflected America's post-war fascination with labor saving devices and television. The introduction of the prepared meals coincided with the first coast-to-cost color broadcast. A test run of 5000 dinner trays was produced in the first place, filled by women using ice cream scoops. The very first meal did indeed feature turkey, together with corn bread dressing, gravy, buttered peas and sweet potatoes. The range was extended to include a choice of classic American dishes (including Salisbury steak, meatloaf and fried chicken). In the original dinners, foil trays were used to separate the food groups into three compartments. A fourth, dessert section, was added in 1960 but this was finally deleted in 2001. One of these original foil trays is on show

Did you know?

- 66% of US households tune in to the TV during mealtimes. This represents a massive shift away from the traditional "family meal" eaten at table.
- When the dinners were introduced, Americans owned 33 million TV sets.
- Women prepare 77% of all American dinners.
- The Swanson 1lb Hungry-Man turkey dinner currently costs c. $3.39.

> *"Women are becoming food assemblers, not food preparers"*
>
> Diane Jacobs, Pinnacle Foods Corporation

at the Smithsonian Institute. With the advent of domestic microwaves in the '80s, the then-owners of Swanson, the Campbell Soup Company, replaced the foil trays with plastic ones.

Swanson's current owner, the Pinnacle Foods Corporation of New Jersey, recently celebrated fifty years of the TV dinner in 2003. It is now more popular than ever, and the company offers 76 meal varieties, including "Mexican Style Fiesta", and "Noodles and Gravy with Sirloin Beef Tips", all served in the familiar three-compartment trays.

More than just a convenient meal solution, the TV dinner has been an accelerator of social change and has helped to change the dynamics of the American family itself. Its cultural value was celebrated in 1999 when it was awarded its own star on the Hollywood Walk of Fame. Swanson remains a $450 million brand.

Victor Victrola

V

Birthplace: Camden, NJ

Originator: Eldridge Johnson

Date Introduced: 1906

Original Price: $200

Model Code: VTLA/VV-XVI

First Year Production: 1500-2000 machines

Production to 1909: 20,000 machines

Yearly Sales 1913: 231,903 machines

Yearly sales 1917: 568,683 machines

When **The Victor Talking Machine Company was incorporated in 1901, all phonographs had horns to amplify their sound.** These were very ungainly, and when they were bumped into, the record would get scratched. Company founder Eldridge Johnson decided to conceal the horn beneath the turntable so that the whole ensemble would fit into a smart wooden cabinet, and become an attractive piece of parlor furniture. Because the Victor Company had no cabinet manufacturing

Did you know?

- Sales of the electric turntable Victrola of 1913 were initially slow. Many homes still lacked main power.
- The all-time best selling Victrola was the VV-XI floor model. Over 850,000 were sold between 1910-1921.
- One of the 2,000 original flat top models, complete with a Pooley Cabinet, can command a price of thousands of dollars.

"The whole mechanism has the simplicity of perfection."

Victrola manual, 1924

facilities, they contracted out the work to the Pooley Company of Philadelphia. These early flat top models first appeared in 1906. In 1907 Victrola opened its own cabinet facility. Their 1911 introduction of budget priced models (priced between $15 and $50) greatly accelerated the company's fortunes. Sales doubled between 1913 and 1917.

Following WWI, several other companies challenged Victrola's market dominance, and sales dipped. Radio's growing popularity in the '20s also depressed phonograph sales. Radio was free and you didn't need to buy records. Victrola fought back by fitting radios in their consoles, which also used the speaker horn. Victrola's Orthophonic model had greatly improved sound quality, achieved by an aluminum diaphragm in the soundbox, and was fitted with a RCA radio. This cooperation between the two companies resulted in RCA taking over Victrola in 1929.

Water Skis

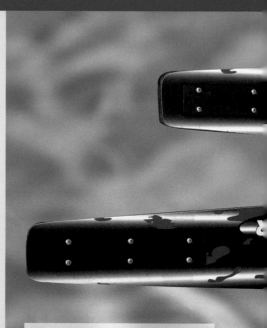

Birthplace: Lake City, MN
Originator: Ralph Samuelson
Date Introduced: June 1922
First Patent Filed: by Fred Waller
Date of Patent: 1925

Water Ski Association Founded: 1939
First Water Ski Championships: 1939
Location: Jones Beach, Long Island, NY
Annual Water Ski Tournaments: 900 plus
Water-skiers in U.S.: 11 million

Eighteen-year-old Ralph Samuelson wondered why, if you could ski on snow, why couldn't you ski on water? He tried out his theory on Lake Pepin, Lake City, Minnesota, towed by his brother Ben. The brothers experimented for several days. First, Ralph tried barrel staves and snow skis—and finally constructed the first crude pair of water skis. They were made from two eight-foot-long pieces of lumber, with leather strips for bindings. He attached a hundred-foot-long sash cord to the boat, and held a large metal ring. After a few days' trials, Ralph realized that he needed to lean back and so stood up for the first time. He went on to make the first water ski jump in 1925 and ultimately managed to speed ski behind a boat travelling at 80 mph. But Ralph never patented his invention. Fred Waller was the first to do that and it was Jack Andersen who went on to invent shorter, finless "trick" skis. Modern skis are made from fiberglass and other composite materials, but Ralph Samuelson would still recognize their purpose.

Did you know?

- Ralph Samuelson's first successful ski was a couple of days before his nineteenth birthday.
- Ralph became known as the "Father of Water-skiing."

"*Ralph Samuelson died August 1977 with the knowledge that what he started back in 1922 was giving countless hours of pleasure and physical conditioning to millions around the world.*"
Water Ski Hall of Fame

- The 1972 National Water Ski Championships celebrated the fiftieth anniversary of the sport.
- The American Water Ski Hall of Fame is located in Winter Haven, Florida.
- Ralph's older sister Harriet helped him paint his first pair of water skis.
- These cracked, so the oldest pair of water skis in the world is his second pair, now housed at the Hall of Fame.
- Ralph broke his back in a construction accident, which brought his water-skiing career to an end.

W Weber Grill

Birthplace: Palatine, IL	Number of Employees: 500
Originator: George Stephen	Hometown Now: Palatine, IL
Manufacturer: Weber Brothers Metal Works	Date Introduced: 1952
	Original Model: The Kettle
Original Product: Metal buoys	Product Price Range: $34.70–$1,999

When George Stephen invented the Weber in the '50s as the first ever kettle-covered charcoal grill, he started a backyard revolution. To this day, it gives the barbecue cook all the convenience of a gas grill with no sacrifice of quality or flavor. In fact, the lines of the Original Kettle are clearly visible in today's classic One Touch model (as pictured). The company has launched many other grills, including the Flamenco, Penthouse, Wishing Well, and Barrel Bar-B-Q models. To this day, Weber makes the most popular grills in the land.

Did you know?
- The first full service Weber Grill Restaurant was opened in 1988 in Wheeling, Illinois.
- Weber restaurants use Weber grills and burn a ton of charcoal each day.

Wheaties

First Manufacturer: Washburn Crosby Co.

Originator: George Cormack

Hometown Now: Minneapolis, MN

Date Introduced: 1924

Slogan: "The Breakfast of Champions"

Original Product Name: Washburn's Gold
Medal Whole Wheat Flakes

Today's Price: $4.59 (12 oz)

Number of Products: 1

Brand Owner: General Mills

Wheaties were accidentally discovered when wheat bran mixture was spilled onto a hot stove. George Cormack both discovered and perfected the formula. Then, Jane Bausman (wife of a Washburn executive) coined its snappy name. Soon after its introduction, the cereal became associated with sports by sponsoring minor league baseball broadcasts. Knox Reeves tapped into this association when he coined the brand's famous slogan in 1933. Wheaties continues to be interested in nutrition and fitness. The brand has supported many great athletes during its time, and received endorsements from such sporting luminaries as Babe Ruth, Tiger Woods, Chris Evert, Michael Jordan, and Johnny Weismuller.

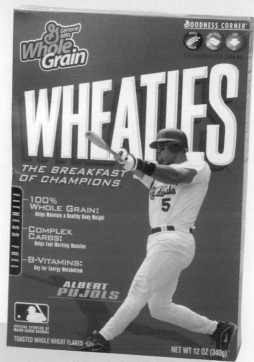

Did you know?
- Michael Jordan has appeared on the Wheaties box 18 times, more than any other athlete.
- Lou Gehrig was the first sportsman to be featured on the Wheaties box.
- Tiger Woods joined the elite ranks of Wheaties spokespeople in 1998.

Wilson Tennis Rackets

W

Birthplace: Chicago, IL

Originator: Ashland Manufacturing Co.

Hometown Now: Chicago, IL

Date Introduced: 1914

Wilson Player: Roger Federer

Original Price: $0.75

Today's Price: From $19.99 to $269.99

Number of Products: 45 rackets plus

Wilson employees: 3062 worldwide

Ownership: The Amer Group PLC

Wilson is the leading brand of tennis racket on the ATP and WTA tours, and provides balls for the U.S. Open Tennis Championship and Davis Cup.** Throughout its history, the company has been at the forefront of technical development of the tennis racket.

Wilson's "n" Code rackets are currently taking racket construction to the molecular level to make stronger, more stable and powerful equipment. Back in the '70s when wooden rackets

Did you know?

- The company was originally set up in 1913 to use slaughterhouse by-products.
- Venus Williams uses a Wilson n4 racket.
- Serena Williams uses a Wilson n3 racket.
- Roger Federer uses a Wilson A Six-One Tour, Natural Gut + Tour Super Six pack racket.

dominated the market, Wilson was one of the first manufacturers to introduce steel equipment, and Jimmy Connors won Wimbledon in both 1974 and 1981 with one of these early metal models, the Wilson T2000. Graphite came next, (such as the Wilson Pro Staff 6.0—still used by Pete Sampras) only to be superseded by Hypercarbon equipment. This is all miles away from the gut-strung "Star" racket of 1914.

"*Wilson ... has developed innovative rackets to deliver power while being kind to the hands, wrist, and arms of aging baby boomers.*"
Popular Mechanics

From the 1930s, Wilson has promoted celebrity endorsements for their products, (including Jack Kramer, "The Father of Modern Tennis"). They now supply many senior players, including Roger Federer and Lyndsay Davenport. Wilson also manufactures tennis balls, ball machines, and a full range of court equipment for the serious player.

W Winchester 1873

Birthplace: New Haven, CT

Originator: Oliver Fisher WInchester

Hometown Now: New Haven, CT

Date Introduced: 1873

Spokesperson: Buffalo Bill Cody

Today's Price: Model 1885, $1,085

Number of Products: 9 individual products, plus variants

Company Name: Winchester Rifles and Shotguns

The first real Winchester rifle, produced by Oliver Fisher Winchester's New Haven Arms Company, was the Henry. Patented in 1860 and produced in 1862, it was available just in time for the Civil War of 1861–1865. The rifle was amazingly modern in all of its details, except for its frontloading magazine. Its key feature was the two-piece toggle link connecting the lever, the hammer, the bolt containing the firing pins, and the moveable carrier. This allowed very rapid fire, with a full 15-shot magazine emptied in only 10.8 seconds. However, it is the Model 1873 Winchester, along with the Colt Peacemaker (launched in the same year), that enjoys the reputation as the gun that "Won the West." John Wayne carried one in *Stagecoach*, and later in *Hondo* and *True Grit*, charging the bad men on horseback and twirling his Winchester with an oversized finger loop. Its classic lines make the weapon instantly recognizable.

In reality, frontier fighting was virtually finished by 1890, and the gun remained in production until 1919, which puts the greater part of the model's output well outside the period upon which its fame rests. The 1873 was an advance over the 1866 model (known as the "Yellow Boy"), as its frame and receiver were made from stronger, lighter steel instead of brass. This enabled the use of the more powerful center fire cartridge propelled by 40 grams of black powder—a truly potent combination. Many famous Americans carried Winchester 1873s, including Jesse James and Annie Oakley;

"I have been using and have thoroughly tested your last improved rifle (the Winchester 1873)...For general hunting, or Indian fighting, I pronounce [it] the boss."
Buffalo Bill Cody

the gun was also used to defeat the "Molly Maguires" in the coal mining regions of Pennsylvania during the mid-1870s.

The Winchester company produced many of the rifles and shotguns used by the American military in World Wars I and II. Today, it is best known as the maker of the

Did you know?
- Lynched lawman turned outlaw Henry N. Brown (1857–1884) begged his wife to sell all his things, "but keep the Winchester." The rifle is now in the Kansas State Historical Society in Topeka.
- The film *Winchester '73* was released in 1950 to celebrate the special edition "One of 1000" guns made by the company from 1875 onwards.
- Charles Goodnight (1836–1929), who blazed the Goodnight-Loving Trail, owned a Winchester '73.

prototypical sporting rifle, the .30-30, used by countless deer hunters. The barrels for these and its other rifles and shotguns are manufactured at a modern factory on part of the original Winchester site in New Haven, Connecticut, and additional components are sourced on a multinational basis.

W Winnebago

Winnebago Motor Homes

Birthplace: Forest City, IA

Originator: John K. Hanson

Date Company Started: 1958

Hometown Now: Forest City, IA

Date Introduced: 1966

Today's Price: $76,290 (Sightseer)

Number of Models in Range: 8

Other Winnebago Brands: Itasca, Rialta

Stock Exchange symbol: WGO

The famous motor homes are named for the Native American tribe of the Winnebago, who wandered the shores of Green Bay, Wisconsin, until the expansion of European settlers. The romance of their traveling life is reflected in the sense of freedom that the Winnebago inspires in its modern owners. John K. Hanson realized that for the farm community of Forest City, Iowa, to survive, it needed fresh industry. So, in 1958, he persuaded a California travel-trailer manufacturer to open a factory. Hanson and five other local businessmen bought the company, which became Winnebago Industries in 1960.

Continual innovation followed. In 1963, a unique lightweight wall construction method, Thermo Panel, was developed and this was instrumental in the design of the first motor homes' launched in 1966. A mere twenty years later, the company had built over 300,000 motor homes. The company prides itself in making everything from scratch. The only exceptions are the engines, which are brought in from both Ford and Workhorse. The Winnebago brand has a very high loyalty factor. Many owners return for up-dated models and sell on their original purchase to the active pre-owned market. This means that Winnebago motor homes have high value retention.

> *"We are very loyal, we trust the quality and we trust the company. I wouldn't go to anything else"*
>
> Bob Ingram, *Traveling Times*

Specifications: The Sightseer (6 Model Variants)

Length: 27feet 11 inches, to 35 feet 2 inches

Exterior Height: 11 feet 11 inches, to 12 feet 2 inches

Exterior Width: 8 feet 2 inches

Wheelbase: 168-228 inches

Weight: 19,000- 6,000 pounds

Fuel Capacity: 75 gallons

Engines: Ford 6.8-liter SOHC Triton V10, developing 310 hp; or Workhorse 8.1-liter Vortec V8, developing 340 hp

World Industries Skateboard

Birthplace: El Segundo, CA

Originator and Spokesperson:
 Steve Rocco

Hometown Now: El Segundo, CA

Date Introduced: 1989

Original Capital: $20,000

Commentator: Steve Rocco

Prices: $36.99 to $144.99

Owner: Private company

In the '80s, most square parents didn't know an ollie from a nollie. This was the secret of the success of skateboarding. Like all worthwhile teen activity, it was a secret club with no adults allowed to be a part. Cool guys hung out on sidewalks; and mall-loading ramps producing satisfying crashing and scraping sounds that made adults grind their teeth. But as with all teen rebellion the participants make the journey to respectability in the end. Avril Lavigne's "Sk8ter Boy," is derided and rejected but ends up as a mainstream rock star. Enter Steve Rocco, Californian skate dude, who scratches together enough investment to start his own skateboard company. Being part of the skateboard scene meant that Rocco could give skater kids what they wanted–and market the boards successfully. Graphics by guru Marc McKee and shaping by Rodney Mullen made his boards stand out from the crowd, as well as helping World to develop a loyal following from this esoteric crowd. World also recruited a line-up of cool pro riders which also boosted their reputation. The hard part for the company seems to have been trying to evolve an up-scale hobby into a business. As founder

Did you know?
- You can choose from models like Wet Willy, Flameboy, or Grinder.
- Least admired board graphics probably include the New Kids on the Block pro model.
- So intricate is World's attention to detail that the wheels are also given a graphic treatment.

"Our whole company has skateboarding in its roots."
Steve Rocco, Founder World Industries

Steve Rocco says: "The challenge is to grow the company to make it a different type of organization." He insists that skateboarding remains "part of the lives of the people who work here." Staying close to their core market will surely guarantee success.

W Wonderbra

Birthplace: Brooklyn, NY

Originator: Sara Stein

Hometown Now: Winston-Salem, NC

Date Company Started: 1927

Wonderbra Launch: 1994

Original Price: $23

Today's Price: from $30

Revenue Sara Lee Apparel 2003: $6.4 billion

Stock Exchange Symbol: SLE

In the 1920s, Sara Stein worked in a bra factory. The prevailing fashion required women to project a flat silhouette and foundation garments had to be uncompromising to achieve this result. Sara decided to design a different kind of bra, which would be popular with women, one that would be designed around quality, performance, fit and comfort. Working on the small Singer sewing machine in her Brooklyn apartment, she made a prototype that would deliver these benefits. Sara's husband, Sam, worked as a salesman for Weber and Heilbrunner, a well-known men's store of the 1920s. His experience enabled him to secure a first-year turnover of $10,000 for Fay-miss, the original name of Sara's company. This was an impressive result for the time.

When they reached retirement in the 1960s, the Steins sold the majority of their interest in the company – called Bali Brassière by this time – to the Hanes Corporation. In 1985, Hanes became the Sara Lee Corporation. In 1994 the company launched Louise Poirier's Wonderbra, amidst unprecedented publicity scenes. A massive 2,800 square feet billboard dominated New York's Times Square, featuring bra-clad model Eva

Did You know?

- Model Eva Herzigova earned around $5 million in 1994, the year she helped launch Wonderbra.
- The current Wonderbra model, Maja, appeared live in Wonderbra's tenth anniversary celebrations in New York's Times Square.
- The first ever push-up bra is thought to be the Rising Star available exclusively from Frederick's of Hollywood in the late '40s.

"They are so brilliant, I swear, even I get cleavage from them."

Supermodel Kate Moss extols the Wonderbra, *Vanity Fair*

Herzigova. It was impossible to ignore. This skilful marketing strategy led to amazing demand. The bras were flying off the shelves at an average rate of one every 15 seconds: Wonderbra's first year sales were worth an astonishing $120 million. *Fortune* magazine proclaimed the bra one of 1994's products of the year. The Steins would have been proud. Indeed, if they were alive today they would surely appreciate that the heritage of their company was being upheld by an on-going focus on well-made, comfortable foundation garments made to flatter the figure in the latest styles.

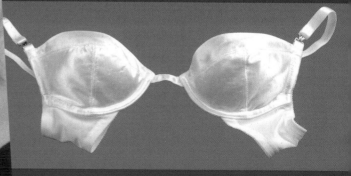

W Wonder Bread

Birthplace: Indianapolis, IN

Originator: Elmar Cline

Date Introduced: 1921

Brand Owned By: Interstate Bakeries Corporation

IBC Headquarters: Phoenix, AZ, and Kansas City, MS

IBC Bakeries: 53

IBC Employees: 32,000

Number of Products: 14 plus

Legend has it that Taggart Baking Company vice-president Elmar Kline was struggling to come up with a catchy name for his new 1½-pound loaf, when he went to watch the International Balloon Race at the Indianapolis Speedway. The colorful balloon canopies filled him with a sense of "awe and wonderment," and an iconic brand was born. The balloon emblem was used to promote the bread from the very

beginning. Children were given balloons attached to letters for their mothers, inviting them to try the new bread. This campaign was hugely successful, and resulted in the brand being distributed countrywide in the late '20s. Wonder Bread has its own hot air Wonder Balloon to this day, in recognition of the emblem's heritage and extraordinary contribution to the success of the brand.

Did you know?

- The "bread enrichment" program of the 1940s eliminated the diseases beriberi and pellagra in the U.S.
- The Wonder Bread hot air balloon began its anniversary tour of the U.S.A. in 2000.
- IBC also bakes another American classic, Hostess Twinkies.

Wrigley's Gum

W

Birthplace: Chicago, IL

Originator: William Wrigley Jr.

Original Capital: $32

Hometown Now: Chicago, IL

Date Introduced: 1892

Price In 1974: 10-pack $0.67

Average Annual Gum Consumption: 190
   sticks per person

Number of Products: 12 plus

Stock Exchange Symbol: WWY

William Wrigley Jr. started his company in 1891 with a modest seed capital of $32. Wrigley first used chewing gum as a sales incentive, and was amazed to find that it was more popular than the baking powder he was trying to sell. Wisely, he switched products and began to market his first two gums, "Lotta" and "Vassar" under his own name. He introduced "Juicy Fruit" and "Spearmint" in 1893, and "Doublemint" in 1914. Over its long history, Wrigley's has continued to add many other brands to its list of products, including "Freedent" (1975), "Big Red" (1976), "Extra Sugarfree Gum" (1984), "Winterfresh" (1994), "Eclipse" (1999), and "Orbit" (2001). Although the company has been publicly traded since 1923, it has prospered under the continuous leadership of four generations of the Wrigley family, including the current Chairman and CEO.

Did you know?

- Construction of the company headquarters, Chicago's Wrigley Building, began in 1920 and was completed in 1924.
- During the war, the company dedicated its whole output of "Spearmint," "Doublemint," and "Juicy Fruit" to the U.S. Armed Forces.
- Wrigley's has almost 50% of the $2 billion U.S. gum market.

W Wurlitzer Juke Box

Birthplace: Chicago, IL

Originators: Farny Wurlitzer and
Homer Capehart

Date Introduced: 1933

First Model: The Debutante

Original Price: $250

Number Sold 1933–37: 100,000 plus

Spokesperson: Milton J. Hammergren

Final Machine: The 1050

Company Ceased Trading: 1975

The history of the jukebox reflects the social trends of the middle twentieth century. The end of Prohibition launched a massive boom in bar-based entertainment, including slot machines, pinball machines, and jukeboxes. During the privations of the Great Depression, the weekends of many people revolved around having a nickel for a beer and another to put in the jukebox. The more affluent could have seven plays for a quarter. The popularity of the jukebox brought it to the attention of organized crime, and in the '40s, Wurlitzer vice president, Milton J. Hammergren, was invited to testify before Congress concerning his links with "helpful colleagues" on the "distribution side," such as mobster Meyer Lansky. In the light of this "distributorship" it is hardly surprising that Wurlitzer dominated the jukebox market until well into the '50s, when their mechanism failed to keep pace with technology. The Wurlitzer's direct competitor, the Seeburg, could play both sides of fifty 45-rpm records, while the Wurlitzer could manage only 24. The company produced their swansong machine in the '70s, the nostalgically styled "1050." Poor sales of only 1600 units caused Wurlitzer's final demise, but the company left a fantastic legacy of wonderful machines.

Did you know?

- Wurlitzer was also famous for large theater organs, which it manufactured in North Tonawanda, New York.

> "We proceeded to reorganize and set up
> a more aggressive distributorship."
> Milton J. Hammergren, Wurlitzer vice president
> on his links with organized crime

- Jukeboxes helped to launch the charts.
- The name comes from the African American word *jook* which meant disorderly or wicked.

X Xerox Copier

Birthplace: Rochester, NY

Originator: Chester Carlson

Hometown Now: Stamford, CT

Original Company Name: The Haloid
Company

Date Introduced: 1906

Xerox Corporation Founded: 1961

2004 Revenue: $15.7 billion

Research & Development Budget:
$760 million

The Xerox is something of a paradox. It is now a commonplace piece of equipment, but it has absolutely revolutionized the history of communication, allowing ordinary people to preserve and share information with ease. Chester Carlson developed a completely original technology that has never been surpassed, and nearly all today's copiers are descended from his "Xerox 914" of 1959. This was the world's first automatic plain-paper copier. Xerox has become a global brand, and is also a synonym for the technology it created. It remains the world's largest supplier of dry ink photocopier machines. Although Xerox's original patent for the basic technology has expired, the company still holds 15,000 original U.S. patents (as of 2002) and devotes 5% of its annual revenue to research.

Did you know?
- Chester Carlson produced the first xerographic image in 1938 at his laboratory in Astoria, New York.
- The first Xerox copier, the "Model A", was introduced in 1949.
- The world's first desktop copier, the "Xerox 813", was launched in 1963.

Zipper

Originator: Gideon Sundback

Employed By: Universal Fastener Co.

Original Name: Hookless Fastener

Zipper Invented: 1913

Zipper Patented: 1917

World's Largest Manufacturer: YKK

Location: Macon, GA

Output: 1,200 miles of zipper per day

Number of Styles: 1,500

Number of Colors: 427

Earlier clothes fasteners, such as Elias Howe's "Automatic, Continuous Clothing Fastener," and Whitcomb L. Judson's "C-curity Fastener" and "Clasp Locker" were pointing the way to the modern zipper, but all still relied on hooks and eyes. Gideon Sundback worked for Whitcomb's Universal Fastener Company and was given the job of taking the concept further. It took him over two years, but Sundback made the first true zipper, with interlocking teeth, in 1913. He called it the "Separable Fastener." B.F. Goodrich used the closure on its galoshes and christened it "the zipper" for the noise it made. Many different types of zipper are now in use, including the coil, invisible, metallic, plastic-molded, open-ended and closed ended. Macon, Georgia, is home to the biggest U.S. zipper plant.

Did you know?
- The average American buys 12 new zippered products each year.
- Zippers took over from the button fly in the '30s.

Z Zippo Lighters

Birthplace: Bradford, PA	Commentator: Ernie Pyle,
Originator: George G. Blaisdell	WW II correspondent
Hometown Now: Bradford, PA	Today's Price: typical brass
Date Introduced: 1932	models start at about $25
Original Price: $1.95	Total Sales: 400,000,000 plus

George G. Blaisdell (1895–1978) was born and raised in the little town of Bradford, Pennsylvania, a few miles from the state line with New York. Starting out as a salesman for his father's engineering company, he went on to set up his own oil business, but turned his attention to cigarette lighters after seeing an acquaintance struggling with an imported model at a Bradford country club. Blaisdell bought the rights to the foreign lighter's U.S. distribution, and redesigned it with a brass case, a hinged lid—and, crucially, a shielded wick that made it easier to use in the wind. He also had the shrewd idea of offering a

lifetime guarantee for his lighters, which he manufactured in Bradford, and began selling in 1932. Blaisdell's company endured some lean early years, but its fortunes received a considerable boost during World War II, when Zippo lighters became treasured items for many GIs. They retained their popularity in peacetime, and even a steady decrease in smoking over recent years has not affected their sales—as over thirty percent of all currently manufactured Zippos are now purchased by collectors.

> *"The most coveted item on the battlefield."*
> Ernie Pyle, World War II correspondent

Did you know?

- The "Zippo" name was chosen as a tribute to another famous Pennsylvanian invention, the zipper (see page 301).
- In their first month of production, just 82 Zippo lighters were sold.
- In 1943, General Dwight D. Eisenhower wrote that his Zippo was "the only lighter I've got that will light at all times."
- Other notable Zippo users have included General Douglas MacArthur, and Ian Fleming's fictional British secret agent, James Bond.
- Though smoking is declining in the U.S.A., Zippo sales have risen over the last few years.

Acknowledgements

The Publisher and Author wish to thank all of the following for their help:
Airstream Trailers: Doug's Vintage Trailers AMF Bowling: Stephanie Darby at AMF Barbie:
Mary Michael Roterman Bass Weejun: David Coles, G. H. Bass
Bell Telephone and Bendix: Magdelena Mayo, Science Museum
Birdwell: Evelyn Birdwell Black and Decker: David Olsen, Comcast
Blue Note Records: Courtesy of the author Burton Snowboard: Burton Snowboard c60s
Cadillac Eldorado: Mike Mueller Carhartt Jacket: Ben Joseph, Covent Garden
Chevrolet Corvette, Small Block, and Chrysler Hemi: Mike Mueller
Chris-Craft: Jim Wangaard, *Classic Boating* magazine Daisy BB Gun: Joe Murfin, Daisy
Museum Disneyland and Hollywood: Corbis Eames Chair: Virta Café, Goodwood Edison
Light Bulb: Leonard De Graaf, Edison National Historic Site Fender: Courtesy of the author
Ford Mustang and Model T: Mike Mueller Formica: The Ruth Harris Collection Frigidaire:
Gord Planiden Gary Fisher Bikes: Josh Vick and Gary Fisher GI Joe: Linda Bessinger, The
Old Corner Store Gillette Razor: Sue Phillips Goodyear Tires: Mike Mueller Greyhound
Bus: Gene, Greyhound Bus Museum Harlem Globe Trotters:
www.harlemglobetrotters.com Harley Davidson: Surrey Harley Davidson Hobie
Surfboard: Mary Michael Roterman Howard Johnson: Howard Johnson Inn, Cincinnati IBM
typewriter: Magdelena Mayo, Science Museum Jeep: Horsham Car Center John Deere:
Andrew Morland/Deere & Company Archive K-Rations: Todd Hogan, Hogan
Quartermaster's Depot KA-BAR: Tara Warner at KA-BAR Kingsford: Hal Frankford,
Kingsford Barbecue Charcoal L.L. Bean: Props by Doug Blackmore Lawn Boy: Christine
Yu, Toro Corp La-Z-Boy: Barmans Ltd., Melbourn Lionel Model Train: Neil Sutherland
Louisville Slugger: Anne Jewell, Louisville Slugger Museum M16: RIA/Robert F. Fischer
Mack Trucks: Bob Martin, Mack/Lehigh Valley Convention & Visitors Bureau Manco Go-
Karts: Jeff Platzer Martin Guitars: The author and Martin website Mesa Boogie Amp:
Westside Distributors Monopoly, Nerf Ball, and Silly Putty: Christine Alexander, Booth
Studio Moog: Magdelena Mayo, Science Museum Oakley Sunglasses: Tony Wilsher,
Larkfield Cycles Pendleton: Cheryl Engstrom Pinball: www.pinballmachines.co.uk Piper
Cub: Chris Foss Pontiac GTO: Mike Mueller Rollerblade/Skateboard: Oddballs
International Ltd. Sawzall: Pat at Milwaukee Tool Co. Schwinn Fastback Bike: Dale Smith,
Moore Large Sears Roebuck: Corbis Smith & Wesson and Winchester 1873: Rock Island
Auction Co. Steinway/Shure: Signal Creative Studio Tonka Toys: Bob Friedland, Bratskeir
& Co. Victrola: Paul Edie at Comcast, *Look for the Dog—An Illustrated Guide to Victor
Talking Machines* by Robert W. Baumbach Winnebago: Dudleys Ltd. Wurlitzer: Graham
Brown and Gus Russo, The Outfit Xerox: Cranbrook Printing Zippo: Linda Meabon,
Zippo Manufacturing Co.